Conversa... TURKISH

IN 7 DAYS

TAYFUN & GILLIAN ÇAĞA

PASSPORT BOOKS
NTC/Contemporary Publishing Company

ACKNOWLEDGMENTS

The authors and publishers would like to thank the following for permission to reproduce copyright material:

Barnaby's Picture Library for the photo on page 57 (top); J Allan Cash for the photos on pages 25 (top), 42, 59; G Payne for the photos on pages 20, 33, 73 and 74; P and P F James for the photo on page 1; Feature-Pix for the photo on page 63; NASA/ Science Photo Library for the photo on page 54; Spectrum Colour Library for the cover photo; Richard Turpin for the photos on pages 7, 10, 15, 25 (bottom), 37 and 64.

All other photographs supplied by courtesy of Tayfun Çağa and S Üçtaşlı.

Library of Congress Cataloging-in-Publication Data
is available from the United States Library of Congress.

Published by Passport Books
An imprint of NTC/Contemporary Publishing Company
4255 West Touhy Avenue, Lincolnwood (Chicago), Illinois 60646-1975 U.S.A.
Copyright © 1991 by NTC/Contemporary Publishing Company
Copyright © 1990 by Tayfun Çağa
Printed in Hong Kong
International Standard Book Number: 0-8442-4565-8

89 WK 9 8 7 6 5 4 3

CONTENTS

INTRODUCTION

Turkish is spoken by more than 150 million people from northwest China to the Balkans in about 26 different dialects. It is an easy language with a grammatical structure resembling that of Latin.

Modern Turkish is written in the Roman alphabet containing 21 consonants (excluding q, w and x) and 8 vowels which are classified as front (*soft*) vowels (**e**, **i**, **ö**, **ü**) and back (*hard*) vowels (**a**, **ı**, **o**, **u**).

Vowel Harmony Rule

The backbone of the language is the vowel harmony rule which dictates simply that if the vowel of the first syllable of a word is a front (or back) vowel, the vowels of subsequent syllables must also be front (or back) vowels. This means that the suffixes added to the words must be formed in accordance with the *sound* as well as with the person and tense of the verb or the function and number of the noun.

Pronunciation guide

1 There are no diphthongs and each letter retains its individual sound. A diphthong is a vowel sound which is made by running together two vowels.
2 The stress is generally on the last syllable of the word.

Back vowels
a as *u* in *cut*: akşam
ı as *e* in butter: ılık
o as *o* in *cope*: çok
u as *oo* in *foot*: uzun

Front vowels
e as *e* in *red*: reçel
i as *i* in *pin*: içmek
ö as *u* in *fur*: köpek
ü as French *tu* or German *über*. Hold your tongue as if to make the *ee* sound and round your lips as if to make the *o* sound: üzüm.

Consonants (similar to English but with the following exceptions):
c as *j* in *jam*:   can
ç as *ch* in *child*:   çay
ğ prolongs any preceding vowel: doğan
j as *su* in *pleasure*:   jiklet
ş as *sh* in *shoe*:   şeyler
v as *v* in *very*:   ve

AT THE AIRPORT

Arrival At Turkish airports, passport control and customs procedures are similar to those at other international airports. You should check your duty-free allowances before entering Turkey. Most Turkish airports have duty-free shops for both incoming and outgoing passengers. There are also currency exchanges for international transactions.

Look out for these signs: **Pasaport Kontrol** (Passport Control), **Bagajlar** (Baggage Collection), **Gümrük** (Customs), **Banka** (Bank), **Çıkış** (Exit).

Hava alanında karşılaşma/ Meeting at the airport

Daniel Daffin and his wife Jill arrive at İzmir Airport. Daniel is greeted by his Turkish agent Tarık Yarımcı.

Tarık: **İyi günler,** efendim! **Affedersiniz,** Bay Daffin **siz misiniz?**
Daniel: **Evet. Benim adım** Daniel Daffin.
Tarık: **Kendimi tanıştırayım.** Benim adım Tarık Yarımcı.
Daniel: Ah, iyi günler, Tarık Bey. **Tanıştığımıza memnun oldum.**
Tarık: Lütfen, bavullarınızı veriniz.
Daniel: Çok teşekkürler.

1

Greetings and introductions

İyi günler	Hello (lit. Good days)
efendim	sir, madam
affedersiniz	excuse me
Bay Daffin siz misiniz?	Are you Mr. Daffin?
Evet/Hayır	Yes/No
Benim adım ...	My name is ...
Kendimi tanıştırayım.	Let me introduce myself.
Tanıştığımıza memnum oldum.	Pleased to meet you.
Bavullarınızı veriniz.	Give me your suitcases.

Polite words

lütfen	please
teşekkürler	thank you (lit. thanks)
çok teşekkürler	thank you very much
teşekkür ederim	I thank you
peki, pekala, tamam	OK
Özür dilerim.	I'm sorry.

EXCHANGING GREETINGS AND INFORMATION

Aile ile tanışma/Meeting the family

Jill is greeted by Tarık's wife Neslihan and their son Cem.

Neslihan: Siz Bayan Daffin olmalısınız!

Jill: Evet. Benim adım Jill Daffin.

Neslihan: Benim adım Neslihan. Ve **işte** oğlumuz Cem. Türkiye'ye hoş geldiniz. **Nasılsınız?**

Jill: Hoş bulduk. **İyiyim, teşekkürler.**

Saying how you are

Siz Bayan Daffin olmalısınız!	You must be Mrs. Daffin!
İşte oğlumuz.	This is our son.
Türkiye'ye hoş geldiniz.	Welcome to Turkey.
Hoş bulduk.	lit. We have found pleasure (said in reply to **Hoş geldiniz**).
Nasılsınız?	How are you?
İyiyim.	I am well.
Ya siz?	And you?
Ben de iyiyim.	I'm fine, too.

Forms of address

In Turkey people generally shake hands each time they meet and also when saying good-bye. There are different ways of addressing people depending on how formal you need to be.

a) If their names are not known:

Bay or Efendim	Mr., sir
Bayan or Hanımefendi	Mrs., madam
Bayan or Küçük Hanım	Miss

b) If their last names are known (formal and polite):

Bay Yarımcı	Mr. Yarımcı
Bayan Akçapınar	Mrs. Akçapınar
Bayan Daffin	Miss Daffin

c) If their first names are known (informal but polite):

Tarık Bey or **Tarık Beyefendi**	Mr. Tarık
Nermin Hanım or **Nermin Hanımefendi***	Mrs. Nermin

* This form of address can also be used for Miss.

Saying Hello . . .

Merhaba.	Hello (informal).
İyi günler.	Good day/hello.
İyi sabahlar (or **Günaydın**), **Efendim.**	Good morning (to a man).
İyi akşamlar (or **Tünaydın**), **Hanımefendi.**	Good evening (to a lady).
İyi geceler.	Good night.

. . . and Goodbye

In Turkish, the person who is leaving says:

Hoşça kalınız.	Good-bye.
Görüşmek üzere.	See you later.

Someone staying behind says:
"Güle güle."   *literally* "Go with laughter."

Introducing your family

İşte oğlumuz.	This (here) is *our* son.
kızımız	daughter
büyük kızımız	eldest daughter
küçük kızımız	youngest daughter
annemiz	mother
babamız	father

annemiz **babamız** **oğlumuz**

	Nationalities	*Countries*	*Languages*
	English **İngiliz**	England **İngiltere**	English **İngilizce**
	Scottish **İskoçyalı**	Scotland **İskoçya**	
	Welsh **Galli**	Wales **Galler**	
	Irish **İrlandalı**	Ireland **İrlanda**	
	American **Amerikalı**	USA **Amerika**	American English **Amerikan İngilizcesi**
	Canadian **Kanadalı**	Canada **Kanada**	
	Austrian **Avusturyalı**	Austria **Avusturya**	German **Almanca**
	German **Alman**	Germany **Almanya**	German **Almanca**

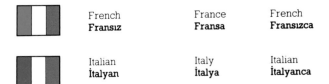

	French **Fransız**	France **Fransa**	French **Fransızca**		
	Italian **İtalyan**	Italy **İtalya**	Italian **İtalyanca**		

Language problems

Ben bir İngilizim.	I am English.
İngiltere'de yaşıyorum.	I live in England.
İngilizce konuşurum.	I speak English.
Lütfen yavaş konuşunuz.	Please speak slowly.
Sizi anlamıyorum.	I don't understand you.
Çok az Türkçe konuşurum.	I speak very little Turkish.
İngilizce bir gazeteniz var mı?	Do you have an English newspaper?

the way it works

People and things

Turkish nouns, adjectives and personal pronouns have no grammatical gender. **Plurals:** words are made plural by adding **-ler** or **-lar** to the singular form in accordance with the vowel harmony rule (see Introduction).

bavul (suitcase)   bavul**lar** (suitcases)
gün (day)   gün**ler** (days)

I am, you are, etc.

Verbs in Turkish usually go at the end of the phrase or sentence. Verb endings change according to the subject of the verb.

The equivalent of the English verb *to be* is **imek** in Turkish. It is a special verb with special uses.

Here is the present tense:

subject pronoun	*verb*		*subject pronoun*	*verb*	
ben	**im**	(I am)	**biz**	**iz**	(we are)
sen	**sin**	(you are, fam.)	**siz**	**siniz**	(you are)
o	**dur**	(he, she, it is)	**onlar**	**dırlar**	(they are)

Ben bir İngiliz**im.**	I am English.
O Daniel Daffin**dir.**	He is Daniel Daffin.
Siz Bay Yarımcı**sınız.**	You are Mr. Yarımcı.

Note The word for *you* in Turkish is normally **siz**, but with people you know well and members of the family use **sen**.

In Turkish two vowels cannot appear in succession, and when this would otherwise happen you insert the letter **-y-** between them:

Ben iyi**y**im.   I am well.

5

Questions and negatives with imek

To put the verb in question form, insert **mi-** (or its variations in accordance with the vowel harmony rule) before the verb ending.

Siz İngiliz **mi**siniz?   Are you English?
Siz iyi **mi**siniz?   Are you well?

If you want to make the sentence negative, insert **değil-** before the verb ending:

Ben İngiliz **değil**im.   I am not English.
Ben iyi **değil**im.   I am not well.

things to do

1.1 Practice saying hello and good-bye to the following people:

1 Mr. Oğuzkan (a business colleague)

2 Mr. Yeşil (your local grocer)

3 Mrs. Köylü (a friend of your mother)

4 Miss Yarımcı (a young girl)

1.2 Now practice greeting your friends:
1 Bay Yazıcı: Say hello and ask how he is.
2 Bayan Özveren: Say good morning.
3 Bayan Akçapınar: Say good evening and tell her you are pleased to meet her.
4 Bayan Yarımcı: Say good day and ask how she is.

1.3 Your name is Mrs. Ayşe and you meet Mr. Oğuz and his friend in the street:

You: [Say hello to Mr. Oğuz.]
Mr. Oğuz: Merhaba, Bayan Ayşe, nasılsınız?
You: [Say thank you very much, you are fine. Ask how he is.]
Mr. Oğuz: Teşekkürler. Ben de iyiyim. İşte Bayan Jale Erkmen.
You: [Say you are pleased to meet her and ask her how she is.]
Mrs. Jale: Ben de iyiyim.

RESERVING A HOTEL ROOM

Accommodations There are many types and categories of hotels (**otel, motel**), varying from the very basic to the luxurious with facilities such as private thermal baths, swimming pools and air-conditioning. Detailed lists can be obtained from the local tourist information offices. Booking in advance is advisable, especially in the summer, and you normally pay for the room per person.

You may be asked to fill out a registration form giving details of nationality (**milliyetiniz**), occupation (**mesleğiniz**), passport number (**pasaport numarası**), and home address (**adresiniz**).

When traveling through the country, look for signs **boş oda var** (vacancies) or **kiralık yazlık** (vacation apartment for rent) by the roadside or go to the nearest **Turizm Bürosu** (Tourist Information Office). There are also numerous **Pansiyon** (boarding houses) whose facilities and prices vary considerably.

7

Bir otel resepsiyonunda/
At the hotel reception desk

Daniel Daffin is checking in at the hotel Yunus.

Resepsiyoncu: **İyi akşamlar,** efendim. Yardım edebilir miyim?
Daniel: İyi akşamlar. **Biz, bir** hafta için, çift yataklı bir **oda ayırttık.**
Resepsiyoncu: Adınız lütfen!
Daniel: Adım Daniel Daffin.
Resepsiyoncu: Bir dakika lütfen. Evet, Bay Daffin. Birinci katta oniki numaralı oda, efendim. İşte anahtarınız.
Daniel: **Odada duş var mı?**
Resepsiyoncu: Evet, duş ve tuvalet var.
Daniel: **Ücreti ne kadar?**
Resepsiyoncu: Sabah kahvaltısı dahil beş bin yedi yüz elli lira.
Daniel: Pahalı değil.
Resepsiyoncu: Lütfen şu kağıdı doldurunuz.
Daniel: Teşekkürler.

At the hotel reception desk

Resepsiyoncu	Receptionist
İyi akşamlar.	Good evening.
Yardım edebilir miyim?	Can I help you?
Biz bir oda ayırttık.	We have reserved a room.
çift yataklı	double bed
Boş odanız var mı?	Do you have any vacant rooms?
Kaç gün için?	For how many days?
Bir/iki gün için.	For a day/two days.
Ben bir oda ayırttım.	I have reserved a room.
... bir gece için	... for one night
... dört gece için	... for four nights
... bir hafta için	... for a week
... iki hafta için	... for two weeks

Ben tek kişilik bir oda istiyorum.	I would like a single room.
... çift yataklı	... a double room
... iki tek yataklı	... with two single beds
... banyolu/duşlu	... with a bath/shower
... telefonlu	... with a telephone
... balkonlu	... with balcony
... ön/arka tarafta	... at the front/back
Adınız, lütfen.	Your name, please.
Bir dakika lütfen.	One minute, please.
Lütfen şu kağıdı doldurunuz.	Please fill out that form.

The room and the price

birinci katta, ikinci katta	on the first floor, second floor
oniki numaralı	number twelve
İşte anahtarınız.	Here is your key.
sekiz numaralı odanın anahtarı	the key to room 8
Odada duş var mı?	Is there a shower in the room?
Evet, duş ve tuvalet var.	Yes, a shower and a toilet.
Telefon ve renkli televizyon var.	There is a telephone and a color television.
Kaç lira?	How much?
Ücreti ne kadar?	What is the price?
... komple pansiyon olarak	... with full board
... yalnız kahvaltı dahil	... with breakfast only
sabah kahvaltısı dahil	breakfast included
beş bin yedi yüz elli lira	5,750 lira
Pahalı değil.	It is not expensive.

Paying the bill

Yarın ayrılıyorum.	I am leaving tomorrow.
Lütfen hesabı verirmisiniz?	Could I have the bill, please? (lit. Could you give me the bill?)
Sanıyorum, ...	I think ...
... hesapta bir yanlışlık var.	... there is a mistake in the bill.
Kredi kartı kabul ediyor musunuz?	Do you accept credit cards?
Her şey dahil mi?	Is everything included?

Numbers 1–10

0	1	2	3	4	5	6	7	8	9	10
sıfır	bir	iki	üç	dört	beş	altı	yedi	sekiz	dokuz	on

Note: When a noun follows a number, that noun is singular not plural, e.g.: iki bira/two beers   üç şarap/three wines   dört şişe ayran/four bottles of "ayran."
(Şişe means bottle and **ayran** is a drink made from yogurt, water, and salt.)

IN THE BAR

Otel barında bir içki/A drink at the hotel bar

Garson: Buyurunuz efendim. Hoş geldiniz.
Ne içmek istiyorsunuz?
Daniel: **Ben bir bira** içmek **istiyorum.**
Jill: Ben bir meyva suyu istiyorum.
Garson: Buyurunuz efendim, soğuk bir bira ve soğuk bir meyva suyu.
Daniel: **Ne kadar?**
Garson: Bin beş yüz altmış lira.
Daniel: İşte. (Hands him the money) Tamam mı?
Garson: Evet efendim. Teşekkürler, Siz nerelisiniz?
Jill: **Biz İngiliziz.** İngiltere'den geliyoruz.
Garson: Burada ne kadar kalacaksınız?
Daniel: Bir hafta kalacağız.
Garson: Çok güzel. İyi tatiller efendim.

Ordering a drink

garson	waiter
Buyurunuz	Come in, Welcome; Here it is
hoş geldiniz	welcome
Ne içmek istiyorsunuz?	What do you want to drink?
Ben bira içmek istiyorum.	I want to drink beer.
şarap	wine
rakı	raki
meyva suyu	fruit juice
maden suyu	mineral water
çay	tea
kahve	coffee
soğuk bir bira	a cold beer
soğuk bir meyva suyu	a cold fruit juice
Ne kadar?	How much?
beş bin yüz altmış lira	5,160 lira
İşte.	Here it is.
Tamam mı?	Is that OK?
Çok güzel.	Very good.

Saying where you are from

Siz nerelisiniz?	Where are you from?
Siz nereden geliyorsunuz?	Where did you arrive from?
Ben İngilizim.	I am English.
Ben Londra'dan geliyorum.	I arrived from London.

Useful words and phrases

ne kadar (süre, zaman)?	How long?
Burada ne kadar kalacaksınız?	How long are you staying here?
Bir hafta kalacağız.	We are staying for a week.
İyi tatiller.	Have a good vacation.

the way it works

How to form words

There are no separate words for prepositions such as *to, at, in, on,* and *from* in Turkish. These words are represented by suffixes – endings that are added onto nouns and pronouns and called case endings.

We have already seen several of these in the dialogues in this unit, e.g.:

Oda**da** duş var mı?   Is there a shower *in* the room? (**Oda** = room)
Ben İngiltere**'den** geliyorum.   I come *from* England.

There are six cases in Turkish, all of which take different sets of endings, except the nominative (subject) case which takes no ending. Don't be too concerned with the cases at the moment. They will be introduced gradually throughout the book.

11

There is/there are

Note the following example from the dialogue:

Odada duş **var mı?**	Is there a shower in the room?

The answer in this case is:

Evet, duş ve tuvalet **var**.	Yes, there is a shower and toilet.

Adding **mı** turns the statement into a question.

Substituting **yok** means "there isn't/there aren't."

Odada havlu **yok**.	There aren't any towels in the room.

Note: **var** is also used to mean "to have" in the sense of availability.

Boş odanız **mı?**	Are there any vacant rooms? (= do you have?)
Odada havlu var **mı?**	Are there any towels in the room?

Verbs

All Turkish verbs end in **-mek** or **-mak** in their infinitive form, in accordance with the vowel harmony rule (see Introduction). The part before the **-mek/ -mak** is called the stem, e.g.:

ver**mek**	to give	bak**mak**	to look
iç**mek**	to drink	yaz**mak**	to write

The present tense

There are two forms of present tense in Turkish – the *aorist* and the *continuous present*. The *aorist* denotes continuing or habitual activity:

Sabahları çay içerim.*   I drink tea in the morning.

*After consonant stems (**içmek** = to drink) a vowel is added before the **r**.

The *continuous present* is used for actions either in progress or envisaged and is differentiated by means of the suffix **-yor-** which is placed *after* the verb stem and *before* the ending:

Çay iç**iyor**um*   I *am drinking* tea

*After consonant stems a closed vowel is added before **-yor-**.

Endings of verbs

Different endings are added to the stem to indicate who the subject of the verb is. The vowel in the ending will be harmonized with the previous sound in accordance with the vowel harmony rule.

gel**mek** (to come)	*Continuous Present*
Ben İngiltere'den geliyor**um**.	*I* come from England.
Biz Fransa'dan geliyor**uz**.	*We* come from France.
Siz İtalya'dan geliyor**sunuz**.	*You* come from Italy.
Nereden geliyor**sunuz**?	Where do *you* come from?

How to say you want something

If you want something use the verb **istemek**.

Ne **istiyorsunuz**?	What do *you want*?
Bir bira **istiyorum**.	*I want* a beer.
Bir oda **istiyoruz**.	*We want* a room.
Ben Amerika'ya telefon etmek **istiyorum**.	*I want* to telephone America.

things to do

1.4 Practice reserving a room at a hotel.

Receptionist: İyi akşamlar efendim. Yardım edebilir miyim?
You: [Say good evening and ask if there are any vacant rooms.]
Receptionist: Evet, efendim. Kaç gün için?
You: [Say for a week.]
Receptionist: Bir dakika lütfen ...
You: [Say you would like a single room with a shower.]
Receptionist: Özür dilerim. Çift yataklı bir oda var fakat tek kişilik yok.
You: [Say that's OK. Ask if there is a shower in the room.]
Receptionist: Evet, efendim, duş ve tuvalet var.
You: [Say that's fine and ask how much it is.]

1.5 You are in a taverna ordering drinks for your party. Everyone seems to want something different.

ORDERING BREAKFAST

Breakfast is usually a light meal consisting of bread, butter, feta cheese, olives and jam, and is served with Turkish tea. It is, however, possible to order a continental-style breakfast in larger hotels. Turkish coffee or instant coffee can also be served on request.

Otelde sabah kahvaltısı/ Breakfast at the hotel

Jill and Daniel are ordering breakfast.

Garson: Günaydın, efendim, buyurunuz.
Jill: **Günaydın.**
Daniel: İyi sabahlar.
Garson: Kahvaltı istiyor musunuz?
Daniel: Evet, lütfen. Benim karnım çok aç.
Jill: Kahvaltıda neler var?
Garson: Ekmek, tereyağı, beyaz peynir, zeytin ve reçel var. Çay, kahve veya meyva suyu içebilirsiniz.
Daniel: **Lütfen bana,** ekmek, tereyağı ve reçel **getiriniz. Ben bir** bardak Türk çayı içmek **istiyorum,** lütfen.
Jill: Lütfen bana, ekmek, beyaz peynir, zeytin ve bir bardak mevya suyu getiriniz.
Garson: Derhal efendim. Afiyet olsun.

14

What's for breakfast?

kahvaltı	breakfast
Kahvaltı istiyor musunuz?	Would you like breakfast?
Benim karnım çok aç.	I am very hungry.
Ben çok susadım.	I am very thirsty.
Kahvaltıda neler var?	What is there for breakfast?
ekmek	bread
tereyağı	butter
beyaz peynir	feta cheese
zeytin	olives
reçel	jam
çay	tea
Türk çayı	Turkish tea
kahve	coffee
Türk kahvesi	Turkish coffee
içebilirsiniz	you can drink
lütfen bana ... getiriniz	please bring me
bir bardak	a glass
Derhal, efendim.	Immediately, sir.
Afiyet olsun.	Enjoy your meal.

AT THE RESTAURANT

Turkish cuisine is world famous and a great experience. There are hot and cold dishes with olive oil, **meze** (appetizers), a great variety of fresh salads and fruits, and many kinds of fish from the Black Sea, the Aegean, and the Mediterranean.

Bir lokantaya davet/Invitation to a restaurant

Jill and Daniel are met by their friends Recep and Tuncay who have invited them for a meal in a Turkish restaurant.

Garson: Buyurunuz efendim, hoş geldiniz.
Recep: Şurada **dört kişilik boş bir masa var.**
Jill: Bu lokanta çok temiz ve büyük.

Tuncay: Evet, yemekler de güzeldir.
Garson: Yemekten önce bir şey içer misiniz?
Daniel: İçecek neler var?
Garson: İşte liste, efendim.
Jill: Ben bir bardak limonata istiyorum.
Tuncay: Benim için soğuk bir kokakola lütfen.
Recep: Bir büyük bira lütfen.
Daniel: Bir bardak Doluca beyaz şarap lütfen.
Garson: Derhal efendim.
Jill: Türk yemekleri gerçekten çok leziz. Ben, bir yayla çorbası, **bir porsiyon** Adana şiş kebabı ve cacık istiyorum.
Tuncay: Ben, çoban salatası, zeytin yağlı taze fasulye ve İskender kebabı istiyorum.
Recep: Karışık salata, yaprak sarması ve ıspanaklı börek getiriniz.
Daniel: Cacık, pilav ve İnegöl köftesi lütfen.
Garson: **Yemekte içki ister misiniz?**
Recep: Evet, 1977 Doluca kırmızı ve bir küçük rakı lütfen.
Garson: Derhal efendim. Afiyet olsun.

Getting a table

Şurada boş bir masa var.	There's an empty table there.
burada/orada/şurada	here/over there/there
boş/dolu	empty (vacant)/full (occupied)
Dört kişilik bir masanız var mı?	Do you have a table for four?
pencere yanında/terasta/ köşede	by the window/on the terrace/ in the corner
Bir masa ayırtmak istiyorum.	I'd like to reserve a table.
temiz/kirli	clean/dirty
büyük/küçük	big (large)/small
restoran/lokanta	restaurant
yemekler	dishes

16

Ordering a meal

Yemekten önce bir şey içer misiniz?	Would you like to drink something before the meal?
önce/sonra	before/after
İçecek neler var?	What is there to drink?
İşte liste.	Here is the list.
İşte yemek listesi.	Here is the menu.

DOĞU İŞKEMBECİSİ VE LOKANTASI

PİLAVLAR	TATLILAR
Pirinç pilav tereyağlı	Fırın sütlaç ......
Bulgur pilav	Keşkül ......
İç pilav	Aşure ......
Patlıcan pilav	Ekmek kadayıfı ......
Bezelyeli pilav	
Meyhane pilavı	Kemal Paşa ......
Fırın makarna	İrmik helvası ......
Kıymalı Makarna	Tel kadayıf ......
....	
BÖREKLER	Revani ......
Kıymalı börek	Kabak tatlısı cevizli ......
Peynirli börek	Çilek komposto ......
Ispanaklı börek	Elma komposto ......
ZEYTİNYAĞLILAR	
~~ıt ciğeri	

bir bardak Doluca beyaz şarap	a glass of Doluca white wine
gerçekten	as a matter of fact
leziz	tasty
bir porsiyon ...	a portion of ...
Türk yemekleri	Turkish food
yayla çorbası	a kind of yogurt soup
Adana şiş kebabı	Adana-style skewered kebab
cacık	cucumber slices in yogurt with garlic and salt
çoban salatası	shepherd's salad
zeytin yağlı taze fasulye	green beans in olive oil
İskender kebabı	döner kebab with yogurt and tomato sauce, cooked in butter

17

yaprak sarması	stuffed vine leaves
ıspanaklı börek	pastry with spinach
pilav	plain cooked rice
İnegöl köftesi	meat balls cooked in İnegöl style
Yemekte içki ister misiniz?	Would you like a drink (alcoholic) with your meal?
Tavsiye ederim . . .	I recommend . . .
Etyemez yemekleri var mı?	Are there any vegetarian dishes?
Ne arzu edersiniz, et mi yoksa balık mı?	What would you like, meat or fish?

Paying the bill

Hesabı getirir misiniz?	Will you bring the check?
Kredi kartı ile ödeyebilir miyim?	Can I pay by credit card?
Servis dahil mi?	Is service included?
Tuvaletler nerede?	Where are the toilets?
Yemekler çok nefisti.	The food was excellent.

Table vocabulary

bıçak	knife	**peçete**	napkin
çatal	fork	**kürdan**	toothpick
kaşık	spoon	**tuz**	salt
tabak	plate	**biber**	pepper
bardak	glass	**acı biber**	hot pepper (cayenne)
kültablası	ashtray	**kara biber**	black pepper

the way it works

A polite command

Look at the following example from the dialogue:

Lütfen, **bana** ekmek . . . **getiriniz.**	Please bring me some bread.
Lütfen, **bana** hesabı **getiriniz.**	Please bring me the check.

This imperative form is very easy to learn: **getiriniz** comes directly from the stem of the verb, in this case **getir-**, to which the ending **-(i)niz** is added.

Lütfen, **bana** . . . **veriniz**	Please give me

Note the position of **bana** (to me) which always goes before the verb.

This and that, here and there

Bu lokanta	this restaurant	**burada**	here
Şu masa	that table	**şurada**	there
O masa	that table over there	**orada**	over there

things to do

2.1 You are with a group of tourists at a Turkish hotel and the only person who can speak the language. The waiter asks **"Ne arzu edersiniz?"** (What would you like?). Can you order breakfast for everyone?

1   Frances: bread, feta cheese, and a cup of Turkish coffee.

2   Peter: bread, butter, and jam.

3   Andrew: bread, olives, and fruit juice.

4   Jane: bread, jam, and Turkish coffee.

2.2 You have arrived at a restaurant. Tell the waiter what you want.
1   Ask if there is a table for four.
2   Ask the waiter to bring you the menu.
3   Ask what there is to drink.
4   Say you would like one soup, one shish kebab, and one Adana kebab with a mixed salad.
5   Ask for a bottle of rakı.
6   Ask for the check.

SHOPPING FOR FOOD

Money   The monetary system in Turkey is the Turkish Lira (TL). The system is decimal. Before leaving for Turkey, it's a good idea to check whether there is a limit to how many lira can be taken out of the country. In most tourist areas major credit cards are accepted.

Shops are generally open from 8:30 a.m. to 1 p.m. and from 2 p.m. to 7 p.m., and close on Sundays except in tourist areas where they can be open from early morning until midnight or beyond.

There are local markets on specific days of the week for each district, where one can buy fresh food, fruit, and vegetables and other requirements.

Pazarda alış-veriş/Shopping at the market

Daniel and Jill are at the local market.

Daniel: Bak, şurada çok güzel şeftaliler var. Biraz satın alalım.
Satıcı: Buyurunuz. Ne kadar istiyorsunuz?
Jill: **İki kilo lütfen.**
Daniel: **Kaç lira?**
Satıcı: Kilosu 750 lira beyim.
Daniel: İşte 1500 liranız.
Satıcı: Teşekkürler, afiyetle yiyiniz.

Buying food

Biraz satın alalım.	Let's buy some.
Ne kadar istiyorsunuz?	How much do you want?
İki kilo lütfen.	Two kilos, please.
Kaç lira?	How much (does it cost)?
Kilosu 750 lira.	750 lira per kilo.
Afiyetle yiyiniz.	Eat it with good appetite.

Useful shopping phrases

bir litre	a liter of
iki dilim	two slices of
bir paket	a pack of ...
fazla/az/çok fazla	more/less/too much
bu/şu	this one/that one
bunlar/şunlar	these/those
yarım kilo	half a kilo
250 gram	250 grams
Başka?	Anything else?
Hepsi bu kadar, teşekkürler.	That's all, thanks.

SHOPPING FOR PRESENTS

It is advisable to bargain politely over the price of large items like carpets and leather goods.

Carpets, kilims, onyx, china, leather, copperware, silk, toweling, herbs, and spices are good items to purchase for value and quality.

Hediyelik eşya dükkanında/
At the souvenir shop

While out window-shopping, Jill and Daniel are invited into a shop by Cüneyt, the shopkeeper.

Cüneyt: Buyurunuz efendim! Hoş geldiniz! Satın almak önemli değil. Bakınız!
Daniel: Teşekkürler.
Jill: **Bu nedir?**
Cüneyt: **O bir semaverdir.** Belki biliyorsunuz, biz Türkler çayı çok severiz.
Daniel: **Biz** küçük bir kilim **satın almak istiyoruz.**
Cüneyt: Burada pek çok çeşitimiz var. Pahalı, ucuz. İpek, pamuk ipliği veya yün elde dokunmuş!
Jill: Şu küçük mavi ve kırmızı motifli kilimi **görebilir miyim?**
Cüneyt: Buyurunuz, güzel bir yörük kilimi!
Jill: Kaç lira?
Cüneyt: Pahalı değil. 150,000 liradır. Değerli ve hakiki bir el sanatı.
Daniel: 125,000 lira verebiliriz!
Cüneyt: Peki, sizin için 130,000 lira.
Daniel: **Peki, işte paranız.**
Cüneyt: Teşekkürler. Güle güle eskitiniz.

Buying souvenirs

satın almak	to buy
önemli değil	it is not important/essential
Bakınız	Please look (at)
Bu nedir?	What is this?
O bir semaverdir.	It is a samovar.
Belki biliyorsunuz	Perhaps you know
biz Türkler severiz	we, the Turks, like ...
küçük bir kilim	a small rug
burada	in here
pek çok çeşitimiz	a lot of different kinds
pahalı/ucuz	expensive/cheap
ipek/pamuk/yün	silk/cotton/wool
elde dokunmuş	hand-woven
eski/yeni	old/new
büyük/küçük	big/small
beyaz/siyah/mavi	white/black/blue
yeşil/sarı/kırmızı	green/yellow/red
kahverengi/pembe/gri	brown/pink/grey
motifli	patterned
... görebilir miyim?	Can I see ... ?
güzel bir yörük kilimi	a pretty Turcoman rug
değerli ve hakiki	valuable and original
bir el sanatı	a handmade piece
... lira verebiliriz!	We can give ... lira!

Peki sizin için ... lira.	O.K. for you ... lira.
Güle güle eskitiniz.	Please make use of it with happiness.
bir seramik tabak	a pottery dish
bir kaç tesbih (taşı)	some worry beads
bir gömlek	a shirt

the way it works

Adjectives

Adjectives in Turkish are placed before the noun, as in English:

küçük kilim	small rug
taze meyvalar	fresh fruits

The indefinite article **bir** can precede or follow the adjective. Depending on the context, it can mean either "a" or "the."

bir küçük kilim	a small rug
küçük bir kilim	the small rug
değerli ve hakiki bir halı	the valuable and genuine carpet

To be able to ...

Look at the following phrase:
Çay veya kahve içebilirsiniz.   You can drink tea or coffee.

To say *you can* you add **-ebil-** or **-abil-** to the stem of the verb before the tense and personal suffixes.
125,000 lira ver**ebil**iriz.   We can give 125,000 lira.

Following the same pattern:
görmek (to see)   gör**ebil**mek (to be able to see)

Here is the aorist present tense of **görebilmek**:

görebilirim	I can see	görebiliriz	we can see
görebilirsin	you can see	görebilirsiniz	you can see
görebilir	he/she can see	görebilirler	they can see

NB   It is also possible to use the simple present tense with **-ebil-/-abil-**:
gör**ebil**iyorum   *lit.* I am being able to see

To ask a question (e.g. "Can I see?") insert the suffix **-mi-** before the personal suffix, not forgetting to put a **y** between the vowels:

görebilir miyim?	Can I see?
bakabilir miyiz?	Can we look?

Accusative case

If the object of the verb is non-specific you do not need to add any suffix:

Biz küçük bir kilim istiyoruz.	We want a small carpet.
Biz elma istiyoruz.	We want an apple.

23

However, if the object of the verb is specific and a single word, you have to add **-(y)i-** or **-(y)ı-** as an accusative suffix.

Şu küçük kilimi görebilir miyiz?	Can we see that small carpet?
Biz elma**yı** istiyoruz.	We want the apple.

If the object of the verb is specific and a compound word, it will take **-(n)i-** as one of the accusative suffixes after the coupling suffix:

Biz şu küçük **yörük kilimini** istiyoruz.   We want that small *Turcoman rug*.
(Here, the first i added to kilim stems from coupling, but the second i is the accusative suffix preceded by the liaison letter **n**.) (See Saturday, page 61 for further details.)

Here is the full pattern of endings for the accusative case:

Last vowel of word	Suffix
a, ı	**-(y)ı**
o, u	**-(y)u**
e, i	**-(y)i**
ö, ü	**-(y)ü**

things to do

2.3 You are in the market buying fruit for a picnic. You like the look of the peaches (**şeftali**) and the grapes (**üzüm**) and you also want some tomatoes (**domates**).

You:	[Say you'd like a kilo of grapes.]
Shopkeeper:	Peki. Başka bir şey, hanımefendi?
You:	[Ask how much the peaches are.]
Shopkeeper:	Kilosu 600 lira.
You:	[Say you'd like a kilo, please.]
Shopkeeper:	Başka bir şey?
You:	[Ask for half a kilo of tomatoes.]
Shopkeeper:	Başka bir şey?
You:	[Say no, that's all and ask how much it comes to.]

2.4 You have been given a shopping list in Turkish. Can you figure out what you are in fact buying?

> 200 gram beyaz peynir
> 1 ekmek
> 1 litre süt.
> 1 paket çay
> yarım kilo pirinç
> 250 gram zeytin

2.5 You are buying presents for the family. Ask for the following:

1 a small blue rug
2 a samovar
3 a large pottery dish
4 some worry beads
5 a white shirt

PUBLIC TRANSPORTATION

Scheduled internal flights link Turkey's major cities. The service is efficient and reasonably priced.

Traveling by **train** may be tiring but is an excellent way to see the country. It is comfortable and inexpensive. Express services are also available.

Intercity **bus** services are by far the best means of travel. They are comfortable, extraordinarily cheap, and reliable, with a superb network.

Taxi fares are reasonable and in all the large cities taxis have meters. When there is no meter, the fare should be agreed on before starting the trip because there is no control on the prices.

The "dolmuş" taxis are a great favorite. These are usually licensed private cars or minibuses with specific routes and recognized stops. The destination is written on the top of the front window. Fares are fixed and collected en route.

Dolmuş durağı nerededir?/
Where is the dolmuş stop?

Jill and Daniel want to go downtown. They ask Tarık how to get there.

Jill: Affedersiniz! **Biz** şehir merkezine **gitmek istiyoruz.**
             Buradan oraya **nasıl gidebiliriz?**
Tarık: Buradan merkez dolmuşları ile gidebilirsiniz.
Jill: **Dolmuş durağı nerededir?**
Tarık: Sağda ikinci sokakta, köşe başında.
Jill: Teşekkürler. Haydi gidelim.
They arrive at the dolmuş stop
Dolmuşcu: Merkez! Merkez! Hemen gidecek. Buyurunuz!
Jill: **Merkez, lütfen. Kaç lira?**
Dolmuşcu: Bir kişi 750 lira, bayan.
Jill: İşte 2000 lira.
Dolmuşcu: Buyurunuz 500 liranız.

Finding your way

Affedersiniz.	Excuse me.
şehir merkezine	to the downtown area
buradan oraya	from here to there
... nasıl gidebiliriz?	How do we get to ...?

Sabahleyin

ÇARŞAMBA WEDNESDAY

Hava alanına nasıl giderim?	How do I get to the airport?
İstasyon(a)/liman(a) ...	... to the train station/to the harbor
... ile gidebilirsiniz	... you can go by/on
Merkez dolmuşları	by dolmuş with destination "downtown"
... nerededir?	Where is ...?
Dolmuş durağı nerededir?	Where is the dolmuş stop?
sağ/sol	right/left
sağda	on the right
solda	on the left
Sağda ikinci sokakta ...	The second street on the right
... köşe başında	... on the corner
Sola sapınız.	Turn left (**sapmak** – to turn).
Bu sokaktan doğru gidiniz.	Go down the street.
dosdoğru	straight ahead
Bu yoldan dosdoğru gidiniz.	Go straight ahead.
dörtyolda/ışıklarda	at the intersection/at the lights
ileride/karşıda	over there/opposite (across from)
pazarın arkasında	behind the market
caminin yanında	near the mosque

Other useful phrases

Haydi gidelim.	Let's go.
Hemen gidecek!	It's going immediately!
Kaç lira?	How much is it?
Bir kişi	one person
Bana yardım eder misiniz?	Can you help me?
yakındır/uzaktır	it is near/far
Plaj ne kadar uzaktır?	How far is the beach?
yaklaşık	about
Yaklaşık 200 kilometredir.	It's about 200 km.
Yaklaşık 300 metre sağdadır.	It's about 300 meters on the right.
Biraz karışık!	It's a little confusing!
Sizin bir haritanız var.	You have a street map.
Biz buradayız.	We are here.
İşte Hayat sokağı.	This is Hayat street.
Evet. Anladım.	Yes. I did understand.
Dolmuş bizi oraya dosdoğru götürecek mi?	Will the dolmuş take us there directly?
Kuşadası'ndan Efes'e gitmek ne kadar sürer?	How long does it take to get from Kuşadası to Ephesus?

Means of transportation

dolmuş	shared taxi	**tren**	train
taksi	taxi	**uçak**	plane
otobüs	bus, coach	**feribot**	ferry
minibüs	minibus	**belediye otobüsü**	public bus
Yürüyerek gidebilirsiniz.	You can go on foot.		

27

Bir minibüs yolculuğu/Travel by minibus

Later that morning, Jill and Daniel decide to travel from Yalova to Termal by minibus.

Jill: **Affedersiniz,** Termal **minibüsleri nereden kalkıyor?**
Yaya: **Solda** ikinci sokak başında.
Daniel: Teşekkürler.
Şöför: Buyurun bayım. Termal'e.
Jill: Ne zaman hareket ediyorsunuz?
Şöför: On dakika içinde, hanımefendi.
Daniel: İki kişi kaç lira?
Şöför: 2000 lira bayım.
Daniel: İşte buyurun. Bizi Termal'e gelince lütfen indiriniz.
Şöför: Merak etme beyim.

Asking for information

. . . minibüsleri nereden kalkıyor?	From where do the . . . minibuses leave?
Solda ikinci sokak başında	at the corner of the second street on the left
Ne zaman hareket ediyorsunuz?	When do you leave?
On dakika içinde.	In ten minutes.
İki kişi kaç lira?	How much for two people?
Bizi Termal'e gelince lütfen indiriniz.	Please tell us to get off at Termal.
Merak etmeyiniz.	Don't worry.

the way it works

Question words

Banka **nerede(dir)?**	*Where is* the bank?
Postahane **nerededir?**	*Where is* the post office?
Otel **nasıl**(dır)?	*What is* the hotel *like?*
yemek	the meal
yol	the road
. . . **nasıl** giderim?	*How* do I get to . . . ?
Ne kadar sürer?	*How long* does it take?
Ne zaman hareket ediyorsunuz?	*When* do you leave?
Ne zaman açıktır/kapalıdır?	*When* is it open/closed?
Kaç lira?	*How much* is it?

Understanding the time

(for a list of numbers see page 9)
Saat kaç?   What time is it?

The reference points for telling the time are the hour and the half-hour:
a) When the time is *after* the hour but before the half-hour, **-geçiyor** is used:
Saat ikiyi on **geçiyor**.   It is ten past two.

b) When time is *before* the hour but after the half-hour, **-var** is used;
Saat dörde beş **var**.   It is five to four.

The most important things to remember are:

Saat on.	It is ten o'clock.
Saat onu geçiyor	It is ten past ten.
Saat onu çeyrek geçiyor	It is a quarter after ten.
Saat on buçuk.	It is half past ten.
Saat ona on var.	It is ten to ten.
Saat ona çeyrek var.	It is a quarter to ten.

If you cannot remember all of these, you can still read the time on a
24-hour digital basis:
on kırk   10:40   yirmi kırk   20:40
Saat on dört otuz altı.   It is 14:36.
Check the numbers on page 80.

To ask at what time something will happen:

a) To fix a time *after* the hour, **-geçe** is used:
Saat kaçta gelecekler?   What time will they come?
Saat biri çeyrek **geçe** gelecekler.   They'll come at a quarter after one.

b) To fix a time *before* the hour, **-kala** is used:
Saat kaçta dönecekler?   What time will they return?
Saat dörde on **kala** dönecekler.   They return at ten to four.

To ask at what time the bus/train/dolmuş/passenger boat or ferry leaves
you say:
Otobüs/Tren/Dolmuş/Vapur/Feribot **ne zaman hareket ediyor?** or **ne zaman kalkıyor?**

İstanbul'a tren **ne zaman hareket ediyor?**	What time does the train leave for İstanbul?
Emirgan'a vapur **ne zaman kalkıyor?**	What time does the passenger boat leave for Emirgan?

And to find out what time it arrives:
Otobüs **ne zaman varacak?**   When will the bus arrive?
Vapur **ne zaman varacak?**   When will the passenger boat arrive?

Here are the names of some places you may find useful:

istasyon/gar	train station	**banka**	bank
postahane	post office	**hava alanı**	airport
danışma (bürosu)	information	**liman**	harbor
cami	mosque	**çarşı**	market
otobüs terminali	bus station	**stadyum**	stadium
vilayet konağı	town hall	**karakol**	police station
kale	castle	**müze**	museum
park/çocuk bahçesi	park		

29

things to do

3.1 Can you ask a passerby:
1 where the post office is
2 where the tourist information office is
3 where the Osman Paşa Caddesi is
4 where the train station is.

3.2 Now ask the person how you get to:
1 the castle   3 the museum
2 the harbor   4 the mosque

train station	**istasyon/gar**
bank	**banka**
post office	**postahane**
airport	**hava alanı**
information	**danışma bürosu**
harbor	**liman**
mosque	**cami**
market	**çarşı**
bus station	**otobüs terminalı**
stadium	**stadyum**
town hall	**vilayet konağı**
police station	**karakol**
castle	**kale**
museum	**müze**
park	**park/çocuk bahçesi**

3.3 You are at point X on the map and you overhear someone giving a tourist some simple directions. Can you interpret for him and say where he is going to?
1 Bu yoldan doğru gidiniz, sonra sağdaki ilk sokağa sapınız. Cami oradadır.
2 Bu yoldan doğru gidiniz. Soldaki ilk sokağa sapınız. Postahane orada, köşededir.
3 Bu yoldan dosdoğru gidiniz. Yolun sonunda, sağda istasyon var.

TICKETS AND INFORMATION

At the bus terminal you will find many companies operating to and from the same destinations. You can choose any one of them, but as a general rule use the most reputable ones since their services are more reliable.

When buying tickets check the destination, departure time, seat numbers, and the number of the departure platform. Because traveling gets very busy in the tourist season, the terminals become extremely crowded, so watch out for your belongings and make sure that you are on the right bus for your destination.

Bursa-Uludağ'a iki bilet/ Two tickets to Bursa-Uludağ

Jill and Daniel are buying tickets to Bursa-Uludağ from a company named **Bursanın Gülü** (the Rose of Bursa).

Jill: İyi günler. **Biz** Bursa-Uludağ'a **gitmek istiyoruz.**
Katip: Hangi gün, ne zaman?
Daniel: **Yarın sabah.**
Katip: Bir dakika, kaç kişilik?
Jill: **İki kişi için.**
Katip: Evet, boş yerimiz var, **saat sabah dokuz buçukta.**
Daniel: **Bir bilet ne kadar?**
Katip: Bir kişi **yalnız gidiş** 3,500 liradır. Bir kişi **gidiş-dönüş** 6,800 liradır.

Öğleden sonra

Jill: Biz iki kişilik gidiş-dönüş bileti istiyoruz.
Katip: Peki, adınız?
Daniel: Bay ve bayan Daffin.
Katip: İşte biletleriniz.
Jill: İşte 13,600 liranız.
Katip: Teşekkürler. Lütfen terminale bir saat önce geliniz.
           Görüşmek üzere, iyi günler.
Daniel: Teşekkürler, hoşça kalınız.

Buying bus tickets

Ne zaman?	What time?
Hangi gün?	Which day?
yarın sabah	tomorrow morning
bir dakika	one minute
Kaç kişilik?	For how many people?
Boş yerimiz var, saat sabah dokuz buçukta.	We have seats at 9:30 a.m.
Bir bilet ne kadar?	How much is a ticket?
yalnız gidiş	one way
gidiş-dönüş bileti	round-trip ticket
İşte biletleriniz.	Here are your tickets.
Terminale bir saat önce geliniz.	Come to the terminal one hour beforehand.
Görüşmek üzere.	See you later.
hoşça kalınız	good-bye

Entrance tickets

Jill and Daniel are at the incredible calcium springs of Pamukkale where the water petrifies as it cascades down the hill, leaving the landscape encrusted with extraordinarily shaped layers of mineral deposits.

As well as the Aphrodisias and Hierapolis ruins, visiting Pamukkale is a must!

Bir bilet ne kadar?/How much is a ticket?

Jill and Daniel are going to the swimming pool at the top of the hill.

Gişe memuru:	Buyurunuz, efendim.
Jill:	Biz havuzda yüzmek istiyoruz. Kaç lira?
Gişe memuru:	Bir saat için 3,000 lira, bir kişi için.
Daniel:	Biz iki saat kalacağız. İşte 12,000 liranız.
Gişe memuru:	İşte biletleriniz. İçeride soyunma odaları var. Lokanta veya büfeyi kullanabilirsiniz. Su çok sıcak gelebilir, lütfen uzun süre kalmayınız. İyi eğlenceler.
Daniel:	Hierapolis harabeleri yakında mıdır?
Gişe memuru:	Bu yolun solundan gidiniz. Hemen göreceksiniz.

33

Buying tickets for the swimming pool

gişe memuru	ticket vendor
Biz havuzda yüzmek istiyoruz.	We want to swim in the pool.
bir saat için	for an hour
Biz iki saat kalacağız.	We'll stay for two hours.
soyunma odaları	changing rooms
Lokanta veya büfeyi kullanabilirsiniz.	You can use the restaurant or snack bar.
Su çok sıcak gelebilir.	The water may seem to be very hot.
Lütfen uzun süre kalmayınız.	Please do not stay in too long.
İyi eğlenceler.	Have a good time.
Harabeler yakında mıdır?	Are the ruins nearby?
Bu yolun solundan gidiniz.	Go along this street to the left.
Hemen göreceksiniz.	You'll see it at once.

the way it works

Adverbs of time

şimdi	now	henüz	yet, still
sonra	later	derhal, hemen	at once
bugün	today	erken	early
dün	yesterday	geç	late
yarın	tomorrow	önce	before
bu sabah	this morning	sonunda	finally
ertesi gün	the following day	o zaman	then
evvelki gün	the day before	geçen hafta	last week
arasıra	now and then	bazen	sometimes
çabucak	quickly	yavaşça	slowly

Adverbs of place

içeri	inside	yukarı	up
dışarı	outside	aşağı	down
ileri	forwards	karşı	opposite (across from)
geri	backwards		

Locative case endings

You may have noticed in the previous dialogue the phrase:
Biz **havuzda** yüzmek istiyoruz.   We want to swim *in the* pool.

This is an example of the locative case which is used in Turkish to express the prepositions *at, in,* and *on.* The endings depend on the vowel harmony rule and are either **-de/-da** or **-te/-ta** (after the consonants ç, f, h, k, p, s, ş, t).

Here is the full pattern of endings:

last vowel of word	*locative suffix*
a, ı, o, u	-da or -ta
e, i, ö, ü	-de or -te

Here are some further examples:
otelde   in the hotel   masada   on the table

things to do

3.4 You want to go to the Hittite museum (Hitit Müzesi) on the slope of the old citadel of Ankara. You stop a passerby to ask how to get there.

You:	[Say you want to go to the Hittite Museum and ask how to get there.]
Passerby:	Neresi ... Ah, buradan dolmuşlarla gidebilirsiniz.
You:	[Ask where the dolmuş stop is.]
Passerby:	Bu yoldan doğru gidiniz. Sağda ikinci sokak başında dolmuş durağı vardır.
You:	[Ask whether the dolmuş will take you direct.]
Passerby:	Evet, müze yolun tam karşısındadır.
You:	[Say thank you very much.]
Passerby:	Bir şey değil.

3.5 **a)** You are at the bus station with a party of tourists, all of whom want to go to different places. Can you ask at what time the buses leave for their various destinations (Efes, İzmir, Bodrum, Kuşadası)?

b) Now, can you understand the answers? Here are the times. Can you say them in Turkish?

	HAREKET	
İstanbul – Efes	9:10	14:00
İstanbul – İzmir	9:30	15:20
İstanbul – Bodrum	10:00	17:45
İstanbul – Kuşadası	10:40	20:15

c) Can you also ask at what time each one will arrive?

3.6 You are making inquiries about buses to Kuşadası.

You:	[Say you want to go to Kuşadası.]
Clerk:	Hangi gün, ne zaman?
You:	[Say this morning.]
Clerk:	Kaç kişilik?
You:	[Say for two people.]
Clerk:	Evet, boş yerimiz var, saat sabah onbir buçukta.
You:	[Ask how much the ticket is.]
Clerk:	Yalnız gidiş 7,500 lira, bir gidiş-dönüş bileti 15,000 lira.
You:	[Say two one-way tickets, please.]
Clerk:	Peki, adınız?
You:	[Give your name.]
Clerk:	İşte biletleriniz.
You:	[Say here are 15,000 lira and thank him.]

AT THE BANK

Banks are open from Monday to Saturday, from 8:30 a.m. to 12 noon and from 1:30 to 5 in the afternoon. Currency exchange offices (**Kambiyo**) at borders, train stations, airports, and popular tourist places are generally open outside banking hours.

Most United States credit cards are valid with a passport. Traveler's checks are also accepted with identification. The Turkish currency is the lira and you should hold onto your exchange slips when changing your Turkish lira back to your own currency.

Bir seyahat çeki bozdurmak istiyorum/ I'd like to cash a traveler's check

Jill wants to buy some Turkish pottery from the state monopoly shop (**Sümerbank Satış Mağazası**), but first they have to change some money at the bank.

Kambiyo memuru:	İyi günler. Ne arzu ediyorsunuz?
Daniel:	İyi günler. **Ben bir seyahat çeki bozdurmak istiyorum.**
Kambiyo memuru:	Peki, pasaportunuz lütfen.
Daniel:	Ah, işte buyurunuz.
Kambiyo memuru:	Ne kadar bozduracaksınız?
Daniel:	**100 sterlin karşılığı.**
Kambiyo memuru:	Lütfen şurayı imzalayınız.
Daniel:	**Bugün döviz kuru nedir?**

Kambiyo memuru:	2,400 Türk lirası, efendim.
Jill:	**Ben** de 36 sterlin **değiştirmek istiyorum.**
Kambiyo memuru:	Lütfen isminiz, adresiniz ve pasaport numaranız. Şurayı imzalayınız. İşte paralarınız, iyi günler.
Jill:	Teşekkürler.

Changing money

banka memuru	bank teller
Kambiyo memuru	exchange clerk
Ne arzu ediyorsunuz?	What would you like?
Bir seyahat çeki bozdurmak istiyorum	I'd like to cash a traveler's check.
Ne kadar bozduracaksınız?	How much are you going to change?
100 sterlin karşılığı.	Equivalent of £100 sterling.
Lütfen şurayı imzalayınız.	Please sign here.
Bugün döviz kuru nedir?	What is the exchange rate today?
Ben 36 sterlin değiştirmek istiyorum.	I want to change £36 sterling in cash.
İsminiz, adresiniz ve pasaport numaranız.	Your name, your address and your passport number.
İşte paralarınız.	Here is your money.

Other useful phrases

Ne kadar yapıyor?	What does it come to?
Vezneye gidiniz.	Go to the cashier.
Onlar size ödemeyi yapacaklar.	They'll give you the money.
paralar	money
İngiliz sterlini	English pounds
Amerikan doları	U.S. dollars
Alman markı	German marks
ödemek	to pay
para yatırmak	to deposit
para çekmek	to withdraw

İngiliz sterlinim var.	I have cash in pounds sterling.
Çek kartım var	I have a check card.
Banka kartım	a bank card
Kredi kartım	a credit card

the way it works

Genitive case

The genitive case is used when you want to say *of* or *'s*. Here is the full pattern of the genitive suffixes.

last vowel of word	genitive suffix
a, ı	(n)ın
o, u	(n)un
e, i	(n)in
ö, ü	(n)ün

Here are some examples:

arabanın	of the car		Ankaranın	of Ankara
Cemin	Cem's		otelin	of the hotel

39

How to say My, Your, etc.

Look at the following phrase from the dialogue:

Lütfen isminiz, adresiniz ve pasaport numaranız.
Your name, your address, and your passport number, please.

These endings (which follow the vowel harmony rule) are examples of the possessive, and may also occur with a personal pronoun in the *genitive* case, as follows.

personal pronoun	word ending in a vowel	a consonant		
benim	çantam	biletim	my	handbag/ticket
senin	çantan	biletin	your	handbag/ticket
onun	çantası	bileti	his/her	handbag/ticket
bizim	çantamız	biletimiz	our	handbag/ticket
sizin	çantanız	biletiniz	your	handbag/ticket
onların	çantaları	biletleri	their	handbag/ticket

Here are some other examples:

benim bavulum	my suitcase	bizim odamız	our room
senin biletin	your ticket	sizin adınız	your name
onun pasaportu	her passport	onların arabaları	their car
benim seyahat çeklerim	my traveler's checks		

Simple future tense

Ne kadar bozduracaksınız?   How much are you going to change?
(**bozdurmak** – to change)

This is an example of the simple future tense which, as in English, is used to express intention. The suffix **-ecek-/-acak-** is inserted between the verb stem and the ending.

Note: The letter **k** between vowels becomes **ğ**. After a stem ending in a vowel the letter **y** is inserted.

Here are some examples:
gideceğim   I'll go   (**gitmek** – to go)
satın alacağız   I'll buy (**satın almak** – to buy)

The negative form of this tense is formed by inserting **-mı, -mi** or **-mu, -mü** between the stem and the tense suffix (satın almıyacağım – I won't buy). The interrogative is formed by inserting **-mu, -mü** or **-mi, -mı** after the tense suffix and before the verb ending (satın alacak **mısınız?** – will you buy?).

Some independent prepositions

As we have seen, many English prepositions are represented in Turkish by means of the case endings (e.g. *at*, *in* and *on* – locative case). However, there are some prepositions that are independent of the verb in Turkish as in English.

Here are some examples:

ile, -le, -la *(with, by means of):* Araba **ile** gidiyoruz. (We are going *by* car.)
için *(for)* İki gün **için** (*for* two days)
gibi *(like)* uçak **gibi** (*like* an airplane)
kadar *(as … as)* senin **kadar** güzel (*as* beautiful *as* you)

things to do

4.1 You go into a bank to change some money.

Clerk: İyi günler. Ne arzu ediyorsunuz?
You: [Say you want to change some U.S. dollars into Turkish lira.]
Clerk: Ne kadar bozduracaksınız?
You: [Say $100. Ask what the exchange rate is today.]
Clerk: 2400 Türk lirası, efendim. Lütfen, isminiz, adresiniz ve pasaport numaranız. Şurayı imzalayınız. … İşte paralarınız, efendim.
You: [Say thank you.]

4.2 Unfortunately you have lost your purse and report it to the police, who need a list of what was in it. Can you give them a list in Turkish (using **benim** + the correct possessive endings)?

AT THE POST OFFICE

If you need to mail a letter or card, it is advisable to go to the post office, since mailboxes are quite scarce and not easy to recognize. Post offices are open from 8 a.m. to midnight.

Postahanede bir konuşma/
Conversation at a post office

Jill goes to the post office to buy stamps and to mail a package.

Posta memuru:	Buyurunuz, Hanımefendi!
Jill:	**İngiltere'ye bir kartpostal pulu kaç liradır?**
Posta memuru:	350 lira.
Daniel:	Ve **bir mektup pulu kaç lira?**
Posta memuru:	İngiltere'ye bir mektup pulu 500 liradır.
Jill:	Peki, **bize** altı tane 350 liralık ve on tane 500 liralık pul **veriniz**.
Posta memuru:	İşte pullar. Hepsi 7,100 lira tutar.
Daniel:	Ah, ve **biz** bu paketi acele Londra'ya **göndermeliyiz. Ne yapmalıyız?**
Posta memuru:	En çabuk özel ulak ile gider, lütfen şu fişi doldurunuz.
Jill:	Gönderen, adı, soyadı ve adresi. Alıcı, adı soyadı ve adresi.
Posta memuru:	Tamam mı! Evet tartmamız gerek. 16,000 liralık pul lazım. Lütfen şu beyan formunu da doldurunuz.
Daniel:	Peki, içeriği, fiyatı, hediye, şahsi eşya.

Buying stamps

postahane	post office
posta memuru	post-office clerk
İngiltere'ye bir kartpostal pulu kaç liradır?	How much is a stamp for a postcard to England?
bir mektup	letter
bir taahhütlü mektup	registered letter
bir paket	package
Lütfen bize ... veriniz	Please give us ...
altı tane 350 liralık pul	6 × 350 lira stamps
iki tane İngiltere pulu	2 stamps for England
Hepsi ... tutar	Altogether, it comes to ...
ve biz ... göndermeliyiz	and we must send ...
bu paketi	this package
acele Birmingham'a	at once to Birmingham
Ne yapmalıyız?	What do we have to do?
En çabuk özel-ulak ile gider.	Express delivery is the quickest way.
Lütfen şu fişi doldurunuz.	Please fill out this form.
gönderen	sender
alıcı	recipient
ad, soyadı	name, last name
adres	address
Tamam mı?	Is that OK?
Tartmamız gerek.	We must weigh it.
16,000 liralık pul lazım.	It needs 16,000 lira worth of stamps.
Şu beyan formunu da doldurunuz.	Fill out this declaration form, too.
içeriği	its contents
fiyatı	its price
hediye	present
şahsi eşya	personal belongings
Posta kutusu nerededir?	Where is the mailbox?

SPECIMEN ONLY

USING THE TELEPHONE

There are international telephone facilities both inside and outside post offices.

Telefon kulübesinde/At the telephone booth

Jill: Affedersiniz, **biz** buradan Birmingham'a **telefon edebilir miyiz?**

Posta memuru: Kolaylıkla, yalnız çok bozuk para gerekiyor. Önce 99 (uluslararası kod) sonra 44 (İngiltere kodu) ve sonra da şehir kodu ve ev numarasını çeviriniz.

Daniel: Çok teşekkürler, hoşça kalınız.

Posta memuru: Bir şey değil. İyi tatiller.

Making a phone call

Buradan ... telefon edebilir miyiz ... Birmingham'a?	Can we telephone from here ... to Birmingham?
kolaylıkla	easily
Çok bozuk para gerekiyor	a lot of coins are needed
önce	first
sonra	later
uluslararası kod	international code
İngiltere kodu	code for England
şehir kodu	area code
ev numaranız	your house number
Lütfen ... çeviriniz	Please dial ...
Ben Londra'ya bir telgraf göndermek istiyorum.	I want to send a telegram to London
Lütfen şu numaraya telefon etmem için yardım ediniz.	Please help me call this number.

44

the way it works

... to England

If you want to say "to England" you say **İngiltere'ye.** Look at the following phrases from the dialogue:

İngiltere'ye bir mektup pulu 500 liradır.   It costs 500 lira for a letter *to England.*

Biz bu paketi **Londra'ya** göndermeliyiz. We must send this package *to London.*

These are examples of the *dative case* which in Turkish is used to mean "to." Here is the full pattern of suffixes, in accordance with the vowel harmony rule:

last vowel of word	suffix
a, ı, o, u	-(y)a
e, i, ö, ü	-(y)e

... from Ankara

If you want to say "from Ankara" you say **Ankara'dan.** This is an example of the *ablative case* which in Turkish is used to mean *from.* Here is the full pattern of suffixes, in accordance with the vowel harmony rule:

last vowel of word	suffix
a, ı, o, u	-dan
e, i, ö, ü	-den

However, after words ending in **ç, f, h, k, m, p, ş, t** you use **-tan/-ten.**

Pronouns

As well as the subject pronouns **ben, sen, o, biz, siz,** and **onlar** we have seen the indirect object pronouns **bana** (to me), **ona** (to him, her, it), **bize** (to us), **size** (to you), and **onlara** (to them) and the possessive pronouns **benim** (my), **onun** (his, hers, its), **bizim** (our), **sizin** (your), and **onların** (their).

It is worth mentioning here the direct object pronouns. These are: **beni** (me), **onu** (him, her, it), **bizi** (us), **sizi** (you), and **onları** (them).

How to say "I must"

Bu paketi Londra'ya gönder**meli**yiz.   We *must* send this package to London.

To express duty, necessity, or compulsion, insert the suffix **-meli/-malı** between the stem of the verb and its ending.

There are other ways of expressing need and obligation which it is useful to recognize and which we have seen in the dialogues:

gerek: Tartmamız **gerek** (It is necessary for us to weight it.)
gerekiyor: Çok bozuk para **gerekiyor** (It requires a lot of coins.)
lazım: 16,000 liralık pul **lazım** (It needs 16,000 lira worth of stamps.)

things to do

4.3 You have gone to the post office to buy some stamps.

Clerk: Buyurunuz, hanımefendi.
You: [Greet him and ask for two stamps for postcards to England.]
Clerk: İşte pullar.
You: [Thank him and ask to be given four stamps for letters to the U.S.A.]
Clerk: Hepsi bu kadar mı?
You: [Say yes that's all and ask how much it comes to.]
Clerk: Hepsi 2,700 lira tutar.
You: [Say here is the money and ask if you can make a phone call to London.]
Clerk: Evet, hanımefendi. Önce 99, sonra 44 (İngiltere kodu) çeviriniz, ve sonra şehir telefon numarasını çeviriniz.
You: [Thank him very much and say good-bye.]

4.4 There are a lot of things you must do today. Can you tell your Turkish friend what they are?

1 buy some stamps

2 send a package to Australia

3 go to the bank

4 change some traveler's checks

5 go to the bus station

6 buy a ticket to İzmir.

RENTING A CAR

efes
RENT A CAR
KiRALIK OTO tel, 14468

Because Turkey is such a large country with beautiful mountain ranges, driving is a good way of seeing it if you have the time. Most of the main roads linking the major cities are good but they get very busy with long-distance trucks and intercity buses.

Car rental is expensive and prices vary from city to city. Turkish firms are cheaper than the usual international companies such as Avis, Budget, Hertz, etc.

Accidents and repairs: If you are involved in an accident, you must inform the police. An official report is necessary for any legal claims, insurance, etc. Most repair garages are very good and are usually situated on the outskirts of towns and cities.

Kiralık oto ofisinde/At the car-rental office

Jill and Daniel have some free time in the morning. They rent a car to drive to the Anatolian plateau.

Daniel: İyi sabahlar. **Bir araba kiralamak istiyorum.**

47

Ofis yetkilisi: Hay hay efendim. Kaç kişi için? Küçük bir Peugeot ve büyük bir Ford Granada var. Ford Granada'da radyo ve kaset çalar da var.
Jill: Fiyatı nasıl oluyor? Günlük veya kilometre başına mı?
Ofis yetkilisi: Gün başına.
Daniel: Peki Ford'un fiyatı nedir?
Ofis yetkilisi: İşte fiyat listesi ve sigorta ücreti.
Jill: Biz Peugeot'u istiyoruz bir gün için.
Ofis yetkilisi: Lütfen bana İngiliz ve uluslararası sürücü ehliyetinizi veriniz. Evet, her şey tamam. İşte arabanın anahtarı. Lütfen benim ile geliniz, arabayı görünüz.

Renting a car

kiralık oto ofisi	car rental office
Bir araba kiralamak istiyorum.	I want to rent a car.
Hay hay.	Of course.
Kaç kişi için?	For how many people?
Küçük bir Peugeot ve büyük bir Ford Granada var.	There is a small Peugeot and a big Ford Granada.
Ford Granada'da da radyo ve kaset çalar da var.	The Ford Granada has a radio cassette player.
Fiyatı nasıl oluyor?	How is the price calculated?
Günlük veya kilometre başına mı?	Do we pay per day or kilometer?
gün başına	per day
Ford'un fiyatı nedir?	How much is the Ford?
İşte fiyat listesi ve sigorta ücretleri.	Here is the price list and insurance cost.
Lütfen bana İngiliz ve uluslararası sürücü ehliyetlerinizi veriniz.	Please give me your English and international driver's licenses.
Her şey tamam.	Everything is in order.
İşte arabanın anahtarı.	Here is the key.
Lütfen benim ile geliniz ve arabayı görünüz.	Come with me and see the car
Depozito ödemeli miyim?	Do I have to pay a deposit?
Arabayı Konya'da teslim edebilir miyim?	Can I leave the car in Konya?

Other useful words and phrases

motorsiklet	motorbike	karavan	camper
bisiklet	bicycle	trafik	traffic
uzun araç/TIR kamyonu	truck	trafik polisi	traffic police

Gas stations usually provide eating and toilet facilities. Garages are not generally self-service, and sometimes young people attend the car to clean the windshield. A small tip (**bahşiş**) is usually given out of courtesy.

In general, repair shops or garages are also attached to filling stations.

Benzincide/At the gas station

Benzinci: Buyurunuz, efendim.
Daniel: **Benzin istiyoruz.** Süper benzininiz var mı?
Benzinci: Evet, ne kadar istiyorsunuz?
Daniel: **Lütfen 25 litrelik veriniz.** Lütfen yağ, su ve lastiklerin havasına bir bakınız.
Benzinci: Tamam efendim. 15,000 lira.
Daniel: Buyurunuz. Teşekkürler.

Buying gas

Benzin istiyoruz.	We want some gas.
Süper benzininiz var mı?	Do you have super?
Ne kadar istiyorsunuz?	How much do you want?
Lütfen 25 litrelik benzin veriniz.	Please give me 25 liters of gas.
25,000 liralık normal benzin.	25,000 lira worth of regular.
Lütfen yağ/su/ve	Please check the oil/water/tire
lastiklerin havasına bir bakınız.	pressure.
Tamir yapıyor musunuz?	Do you do repairs?
Lütfen lastiklere biraz hava basınız.	Please put some air into the tires.
Buraya park edebilir miyim?	Can I park here?
oto park	parking lot
Burada park yapmak yasaktır.	Parking is prohibited here.

A BREAKDOWN

Araba çalışmıyor!/The car won't start!

On their journey, they stop to rest at a picnic area. When they return to their car, it won't start. After checking the basics they decide to get a mechanic from a local garage and they walk to a nearby village.

Daniel:	Merhaba, bir araba ustası arıyoruz.
Köylü:	Merhaba. Şu köşede Tarık Usta var.
Jill:	Teşekkürler.
Tarık Usta:	Buyurunuz, ne istediniz?
Daniel:	**Arabamız** az ileride yolda **bozuldu**. Bir bakar mısınız?
Tarık Usta:	Hay hay, benim arabam ile gidelim.
Tarık Usta:	Sizin marş motoru bozuk. Değiştirmek gerekiyor.
Daniel:	Peki, **onarabilir misiniz?**
Tarık Usta:	Evet, yedek parçamız var, fakat 45,000 liradır.
Daniel:	Peki, lütfen tamir ediniz, işte parası, yalnız bize fatura veriniz.

Problems with the car
(for parts of the car see page 84)

Bir araba ustası arıyoruz.	We are looking for a mechanic.
Şu köşede ... var.	At that corner; there is ...
Tarık Usta	Master Tarık (**Usta**—master of a trade or craft)
Ne istediniz?	What did you want?
Arabamız ... bozuldu.	Our car has broken down.
az ileride yolda	on the road, a little away from here
Bir bakar mısınız?	Will you take a look?
Hay hay, benim arabam ile gidelim.	O.K., let's go in my car.

Sabahleyin

Sizin marş motoru bozuk.	Your starter motor is faulty.
Değiştirmek gerekiyor.	It is necessary to change it.
Onarabilir misiniz?	Can you fix it?
Yedek parçamız var.	We've got the spare part.
tamir ediniz	please repair (it)
fakat/yalnız	but/only
Bize bir fatura veriniz.	Please give us a receipt.

Other useful phrases

Benzinimiz tükendi.	We have run out of gas.
Bir tekerlek patlak.	One of the tires has a puncture.
Araba niçin çalışmıyor?	Why is the car not working?
Bilmiyorum.	I don't know.
Motor/su/yağ/akü-yü kontrol etmeliyim.	I must check the engine/water/oil/battery.
yağ pompası	the oil pump
vites kutusu	the gearbox
gaz kablosu	the accelerator cable
kayış	the fan belt
... kırık	... is broken
... kopuk	... has broken apart
... çalışmıyor	... does not work

the way it works

Infinitive as subject

Look at the following phrase from the dialogue:
değiştirmek gerekiyor   it is necessary to change

As in English the infinitive can be used as a subject of the verb. Here are some other examples:

İzmir'den **gitmek** kolaydır.	It is easy to go from Izmir.
Telefon **etmek** kolaydır.	It is easy to telephone.

Simple past tense

Arabamız bozul**du**.   Our car *has broken down.* (**bozulmak** – to break down)

This is an example of the past tense. This tense is formed by inserting the suffix -**di**- (or **dı, du, dü** according to the vowel harmony rule) between the stem and the ending of the verb. This suffix becomes -**tı**-/-**tu**- (or -**ti**/-**tü**) after an unvoiced consonant.

Here are some further examples:

Ben yap**tı**m.	I did. (**yapmak** – to do)
Bir araba kirala**dı**k.	We rented a car. (**kiralamak** – to rent)
İzmir'den git**ti**.	He went from Izmir. (**gitmek** – to go)
Ne iste**di**niz?	What did you want? (**istemek** – to want)

things to do

5.1 You are renting a car.
1 Say you would like a small car.
2 Ask how much it costs for three days.
3 Ask if you have to pay a deposit.
4 Say you'll take the Peugeot and ask for the key.
5 Ask if you can leave the car in Antalya.

5.2 You are at the gas station.
1 Ask for 30 liters of super.
2 Ask the attendant to check the tire pressure.
3 Ask if they do repairs.
4 Say you want to buy a fan belt.
5 Ask for a receipt.

5.3 What do the following signs mean:

5.4 Your car has broken down. Can you:
1 Ask someone where there is a garage.
2 Tell the mechanic you have broken down.
3 Say you have run out of gas.
4 Ask if the mechanic will come and look.

ACCIDENTS AND EMERGENCIES

Before traveling to Turkey, check whether you need any special inoculations. It is advisable to have a full health-insurance policy. If you use drugs on a regular basis it is advisable to take enough medication with you. Most doctors speak English.

Nationals of countries with which Turkey has bilateral agreements are treated free of charge. Other foreign nationals have to pay small clinic fees at state hospitals (**hastahane**) and university hospitals. Some private and foreign hospitals are also available but their fees are usually very high. The Turkish medical profession is highly regarded, and doctors are well trained. You can get information about pharmacies on night duty (**nöbetçi eczane**) by dialing 001. You can also get all basic items of healthcare, cosmetics, toiletries, and basic drugs like aspirin, from the pharmacy (**eczane**).

Bir kaza/An accident

While trying to reach the suitcase on top of the closet, Daniel slips and falls off the chair. Jill is out, but the receptionist hears the noise.

Resepsiyoncu:	Bu gürültü nedir? Ne oldu?
Daniel:	**Yardım et**, sandalyeden düştüm. Korkarım ayak bileğimi incittim.
Resepsiyoncu:	Eyvah, nasıl çok ağrıyor mu?
Daniel:	Evet, **bir araba bul**. Polikliniğe gidelim.

An accident

Bu gürültü nedir?	What is this noise?
Ne oldu?	What has happened?
Yardım et!	Help!
Düştüm.	I fell over.
Sandalyeden düştüm.	I fell off the chair.
Korkarım ...	I fear that ...
... ayak bileğim	... my ankle
nasıl çok ağrıyor mu?	Does it hurt very much?
Bir araba çağır/bul.	Get a car.
Polikliniğe gidelim.	Let's go to the clinic.

Bölge polikliniğinde/At the clinic

Doktor: Geçmiş olsun. Ne oldu?
Daniel: Düştüm ve sanırım ayak bileğimi incittim.
Doktor: Bir dakika, neresi ağrıyor?
Daniel: Evet, **tam orası çok ağrıyor.**
Doktor: Hemşire hanım, lütfen bir ayak bileği röntgeni
çektiriniz, ve bir ağrı kesici iğne yapınız.
Daniel: Lütfen bana iğne yerine hap veriniz.
Hemşire: Peki.
Doktor: Üzülmeyiniz, kırık yok, yalnız burkulma var. Size şu
reçeteyi veriyorum, bir eczaneden alınız. Geçmiş olsun.

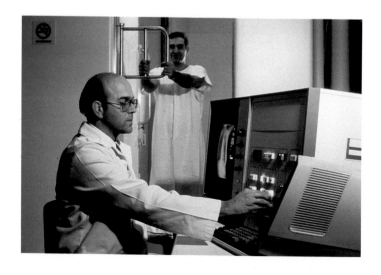

Diagnosis
(for parts of the body see page 83)

Sanırım . . .	I think that . . .
Neresi ağrıyor?	Where does it hurt?
Tam orası çok ağrıyor.	Right there it hurts badly.
Hemşire hanım, . . .	Nurse, . . .
Bir ayak bileği röntgeni çektiriniz.	Have an X ray taken of the ankle.
Bir ağrı kesici iğne yapınız.	Give a pain-killing injection.
iğne	injection
Bana . . . hap veriniz.	Give me a tablet.
yerine	instead of
Üzülmeyiniz.	Please don't worry.
Kırık yok.	There is nothing broken.
Yalnız burkulma var.	It is only twisted.
Size şu reçeteyi veriyorum.	I am giving you this prescription.
Lütfen bir eczaneden alınız.	Please get it from a pharmacist.
Geçmiş olsun.	May you make a fast recovery.

Eczanede/At the pharmacy

Eczacı: Buyurunuz, ne istiyorsunuz?
Jill: İyi günler, **şu ilaçlar sizde var mı?**
Eczacı: Bir dakika, evet hepsi var. Bu ağrı kesicidir. Günde üç
         defa alacaksınız ve bu da adele kremi, lütfen az olarak ağrıyan
         yere sürünüz.
Jill: Çok teşekkürler, işte paranız.

At the pharmacy
(for a list of toiletries, etc., see page 81)

Şu ilaçlar sizde var mı?	Do you have these drugs?
ilaçlar	drugs
Hepsi var.	Everything is here.
Bu bir ağrı kesicidir.	This is a painkiller.
Günde üç defa bir adet alacaksınız	Take one three times a day
. . . yemeklerden önce/sonra.	. . . before/after meals.
Bu bir adele kremi.	This is a muscle cream.
Lütfen ağrıyan yere sürünüz.	Please apply it where it hurts.

Other useful phrases

Yaralımı sınız?	Are you hurt?
Ağrım var.	I am in pain.
Hastayım.	I am ill.
röntgen filmi	X ray
Bir doktor/dişçi/hastabakıcı/-ya gerek var.	A doctor/dentist/nurse is needed.
En yakın poliklinik nerededir?	Where is the nearest clinic?
En yakın eczane nerededir?	Where is the nearest pharmacy?
Baş ağrısı için bir şeyiniz var mı?	Have you got something for a headache?
Boğazım ağrıyor.	I have a sore throat.
İshal oldum.	I have diarrhea.
İshal için bir şeyiniz var mı?	Have you got something for diarrhea?
Günde kaç tane almalıyım?	How many do I have to take per day?
Kaç defa almalıyım . . .	How many times' do I have to take . . . ?
. . . üç defa	. . . three times
Midem de hazımsızlık var.	I have indigestion.
Saman nezlesi olurum.	I have hay fever.
Nefes ala mıyorum	I can't breathe.
uyuyamıyorum	sleep
Midem bulandı.	I've been sick.
Midem ağrıyor.	I have a stomachache.
Başım . . .	a headache
Kulağım . . .	an earache
Dişim . . .	a toothache
Sırtım . . .	a backache
Gözümde bir şey var.	I've got something in my eye.
Elimi/Kolumu yaktım.	I have burned my hand/arm.
Benim . . . ağrıyor.	My . . . hurts.
Benim bileğim şişti/ kırıldı/incindi.	My wrist is swollen/ broken/sprained.
Sıcak/soğuk hissediyorum.	I feel hot/cold.
Güneşte yandım.	I have a sunburn.
Ben diyabetiğim/astımlıyım.	I am diabetic/asthmatic.
Ben doğum kontrol hapı alıyorum.	I am on the pill.
Ben hamileyim.	I am pregnant.
Penisiline karşı alerjim var.	I'm allergic to penicillin.

Other emergencies

If you are in trouble, go to the nearest police station (**Karakol**) or the embassy (**Elçilik**), or ask for help at the hotel.

Karakol nerededir?	Where is the police station?
Acil hastahanesi nerededir?	Where is the emergency hospital?
Bir kaza oldu.	There has been an accident.
Polis çağırınız.	Call the police.
sigorta şirketi	insurance company
Sizin hatanızdı.	It was your fault.

Disaster! *(Acil durumlar!)*

İmdat! or **Yardım!**	Help!
Polis!	Police!
Acil Hastahanesi	Emergency Hospital
Trafik Hastahanesi	Traffic Accident Hospital
Doğum hastahanesi	Maternity Hospital
İlk Yardım/Ambülans	First Aid/Ambulance
Tehlike	Danger
Yangın var	Fire
Dikkat	Caution
Yüzme simidi	Lifejacket
Yangın söndürücü	Fire extinguisher
İtfaiye	Fire department

SOLMAZ-KILIÇTEPE
POLİS KARAKOLU

Loss and Theft

Biletimi kaybettim.	I've lost my ticket.
Anahtarımı ...	my key
Fotoğraf makinemi ...	my camera
Pasaportumu ...	my passport
Çek kartımı ...	my check card
Biletim çalındı.	My ticket was stolen.
Radyom ...	My radio ...
El çantam ...	My purse ...
Kayboldum.	I am lost.
kayıp eşya ofisi	lost and found

things to do

5.5 You have an upset stomach and you go to the pharmacist for advice.

Pharmacist: Yardım edebilir miyim?
You: [Ask her if she has something for diarrhea.]
Pharmacist: Bu haplar çok iyidir.
You: [Say OK you'll take them and ask how many a day
               you should take.]
Pharmacist: Günde dört defa ikişer hap.
You: [Say thank you and ask how much they are.]

5.6 Neresi ağrıyor? Various guests at your hotel are suffering from a
number of ailments. Can you explain to the doctor what is wrong with
each of them?

Kate: David: Peter: Maggie:
sunburn   stomachache   sprained ankle   burned arm

And finally, can you explain what happened to you? You fell on the
beach and injured your knee.

5.7 Here are some of the things that you and your family have lost.
Can you tell the police what each of them is in Turkish? Use ...
kaybettim.

SPORTS AND LEISURE

In the coastal areas, facilities for sea sports and activities may include fishing, sailing and windsurfing, scuba diving, and waterskiing. In the mountains you will find many resorts for mountaineering, skiing, and hunting. There are few restrictions on sports like fishing and hunting but it is advisable to check with the local information office beforehand.

Hangi sporları yaparsınız/ What sports do you play?

Daniel's ankle is much better and he and Jill have challenged each other to a game of tennis on the hotel tennis court.

Cüneyt: Buyurunuz Bay Daffin, ne istiyorsunuz?
Daniel: İyi günler Cüneyt Bey, biz bu öğleden sonra tenis oynamak istiyoruz. Tenis sahası boş mu acaba?
Cüneyt: Bir dakika. Evet işte listemiz, **saat kaç için**?
Daniel: Saat dört gibi, olabilir mi?
Cüneyt: Şanslısınız, boş, efendim. Lütfen dörde beş kala gelip sahanın anahtarını benden alınız.
Jill: Çok teşekkürler.

Making arrangements

bu öğleden sonra	this afternoon
Biz . . . tenis oynamak istiyoruz.	We want to play tennis.
Tenis sahası boş mu acaba?	We wonder if the tennis court is available?
İşte listemiz.	Here is our list.
Saat kaç için?	At what time?
Saat dört gibi, olabilir mi?	Can it be about four o'clock?
Şanslısınız.	You are lucky.
dörde beş kala gelip	about five to four
Sahanın anahtarını benden alınız.	Come and get the key to the court from me.

Other useful phrases

Ben sporu severim.	I like sports.
Ben futbol oynamasını severim.	I like playing soccer.
golf	golf
tenis	tennis
basketbol	basketball
masa topu	table tennis
Ben yüzmeyi severim.	I like swimming.
koşmayı	jogging
ata binmeyi	horseback riding
yelkenciliği	sailing
kayak yapmayı	skiing
su kayağı yapmayı	waterskiing
yürümeyi	walking
Ben spor seyretmesini severim.	I like watching sports.

Ben futbol seyretmesini severim.	I like watching soccer.
Bir stadyum var.	There is a stadium.
Stadyum nerededir?	Where is the stadium?
basketbol sahası	basketball court
voleybol sahası	volleyball court
tenis sahası	tennis court
yüzme havuzu	swimming pool
Bir tenis raketi istiyorum.	I want a tennis racket.
bir tenis topu	a tennis ball

the way it works

Word coupling

If you want to use two nouns together, the case endings depend on whether the relationship between them is **(a)** merely descriptive (*tennis court*) or **(b)** grammatically linked (*the keys to the court*) where the first noun actually belongs to the second.

a) The first noun is in its nominative form (i.e. with no ending) and the second takes the *accusative* case ending (see Tuesday, page 24).

Examples of this construction include:

dolmuş dura**ğı**	dolmus stop
çay barda**ğı**	teacup

and in this unit:

tenıs saha**sı**	tennis court

b) The first noun appears with a *genitive* suffix (see Thursday, page 39) and the second takes the accusative ending.

Examples of this construction include:

bavul**un** anahtar**ı**	the keys of the suitcase
	(lit. of the suitcase the keys)
ev**in** merdivenler**i**	the stairs of the house
	(lit. of the house the stairs)
palto**nun** düğme**si**	the button of the coat
	(lit. of the coat the button)

and in this unit:

tenıs saha**sının** anahtar**ı**	the keys of the tennis court
	(lit. of the court the keys)

Compare this construction with the possessive on page 40.

Exclamations

Here is a list of some of the words used to express emotion or wishes, or simply to attract someone's attention.

A, hah!	Hey! Oh! Ha!
Ay!	Oh!
Aman!	What a shame! Oh dear!
Haydi!	Come on!
Of!	Ugh!
Ya!	Is that so? Really?
Ne!	What?
Hey!	Hey!
Yahu!	Oh, no! (reproachfully)
Yazık!/Vah vah!	What a pity!
Allah Allah!	Good heavens!
Maşallah!	Wonderful!
İnşallah!	God willing!
Aferin!	Well done!
Hay hay!	Certainly, by all means!

things to do

6.1 Can you say whether you like the following sports?
Use either **Ben ... severim** (I like), **Ben ... oynamasını severim**
(I like playing) or **Ben ... seyretmesini severim** (I like watching):

1 tenis

2 futbol

3 yelkencilik

4 kayak yapma

5 golf

6 ata binme

7 yüzme

8 yürüme

6.2 You want to play tennis and you have arrived at a sports complex with a friend.

You: [Say you want to play tennis and ask the person in charge if there is a tennis court available.]

Attendant: Bir dakika. Saat kaç için oynamak istiyorsunuz?

You: [Say this morning at about eleven.]

Attendant: Şanslısınız, boş, efendim. Lütfen, sahanın ahahtarını benden alınız.

You: [Say that's fine. Say you'd like to rent some tennis balls.]

6.3 Ask where to go to watch the following sports events:
1 soccer game
2 swim meet
3 waterskiing competition
4 basketball tournament.

ENTERTAINMENT

Bir açık hava eğlencesi/
An open-air concert

Jill and Daniel have been given free tickets to an open-air concert in town for this evening.

Cem: Haydi **çabuk olunuz!** Konser saat yirmi birde başlayacak.
Jill: Peki, **işte hazırım.**
Daniel: Bir dakika! Ceketimi almalıyım.

They enter the open-air concert area.

Jill: Aman Allah! Çok kalabalık.
Daniel: Programda neler var?
Cem: Konser Türk halk müziği ile başlayacak. Sonra Türk sanat müziğinden şarkılar var. Daha sonra, Türk hafif müziğinden örnekler sunulacak.
Jill: Folklor ekibi var mı?
Cem: Evet, onlar da Türk oyunları sunacaklar.
Daniel: Değişik çalgı aletleri var. Bize adlarını söyler misin?
Cem: Pekala. Saz, davul, zurna halk müziğinde kullanılır. Ud, cümbüş, tambur, saz, keman ve kanun, darbuka sanat müziğinde görülür. Hafif müzikte gitar, elektronik piyano, davullar vardır.
Jill: Susalım program başlıyor ...

Listening to music

Çabuk olunuz.	Hurry up./Be quick.
Konser saat yirmi birde başlayacak.	The concert is going to start at twenty-one hours.
İşte hazırım.	Here, I am ready.
Ceketimi almalıyım!	I must take my jacket!
Çok kalabalık.	It's very crowded.
Programda neler var?	What is on the program?
Konser ... başlayacak	The concert will begin ...
... Türk halk müziği ile ...	... with Turkish folk music
sonra/daha sonra	afterwards/after that
şarkı/oyun	song/dance
Türk sanat müziğinden şarkılar var.	There are songs from Turkish classical music.
Türk hafif müziğinden örnekler	examples of Turkish pop music
... sunulacak	... will be performed
Bir folklor ekibi var mı?	Is there a folk group?
Onlar da Türk oyunları sunacaklar.	They will also perform some Turkish dances.
Değişik çok çalgı aletleri var.	There are many kinds of instruments.
Bize adlarını söyler misin?	Can you give us their names?
Saz, davul ve zurna ...	Lute, drum and flute ...
... folklor müziğinde kullanılır	... are used in folk music
Ud, çümbüş, tambur,	Ud, dulcimer, lute,
keman ve kanun, darbuka,	violin, zither, tom-tom.
gitar, elektronik piyano	guitar, electronic keyboard
... kullanılır	... is used
... görülür	... is seen
Susalım!	Let's be quiet, hush!
Program başlıyor.	The show is starting.

Yemekli bir gazinoda/Dinner at a casino

Later, Jill, Esra, Daniel, and Cem are dining out at a Turkish
taverna, where there is live music and belly dancing.

Jill: Dansöz çok güzel dans ediyor.
Cem: Haydi biz de katılalım. ...
Dansöz: Gel canım gel! Şöyle kalça atacağız. Tamam oluyor.
Jill: Böyle dans etsem, çok kilo kaybederim.
Cem: Aferin, çok güzel.
Esra: Nasıl hoşuna gittimi, ne düşünüyorsun?
Jill: Evet, hoşuma gitti. Kilo kaybetmek için iyi bir yöntem.

Let's dance!

dansöz	belly dancer
Dansöz çok güzel dans ediyor.	The belly dancer is dancing very well.
Haydi biz de katılalım!	Let's join in as well!
Gel canım gel!	Come here, my dear!
Şöyle kalça atacağız.	We wiggle our hips like this.
Tamam oluyor.	That's fine.
Böyle dans etsem, çok kilo kaybederim!	If I dance like this, I'll lose a lot of weight!
Aferin, çok güzel!	Well done, very good!
Nasıl hoşuna gittimi?	Did you like it?
Ne düşünüyorsun?	What do you think?
Kilo kaybetmek için güzel bir yöntem.	It's a very good way of losing weight.

65

the way it works

The passive

Look at these expressions from the first dialogue:
Saz, davul ve zurna ... **kullanılır.**   Lute, drum and flute ... are used.
Keman darbuka ... **görülür.**   Violin and tom-tom ... are seen.

These are examples of the Turkish passive, which is formed by adding -**il**-, -**ıl**- or -**ul**-, -**ül**- to the verb stem, after all consonants except l.
sevmek (to love)   sevilmek (to be loved)
görmek (to see)   görülmek (to be seen)
kullanmak (to use)   kullanılmak (to be used)

Verbs that end in -l and/or a vowel have the passive suffix -**in**- or -**n**-:
almak (to take)   alınmak (to be taken)
okumak (to read)   okunmak (to be read)
Note: examples of the passive are also to be found in the dialogue in Unit 5, page 54: kırıldı = is broken, incindi = is sprained, çalındı = is stolen.

Conditional sentences

Jill says these words in the second dialogue:
Ben böyle dans edersem, çok kilo kaybederim.   If I dance like this I will lose a lot of weight.

Here the verb is **dans etmek**. The suffix -**r**- indicates that it is in the aorist tense. The -**se**- suffix which follows indicates the conditional mode and the -**m** indicates the first person I.

Here is another example:
Akşam erken gelirseniz sinemaya gideriz.   If you come early tonight, we can go to the movies.

Let's ... !

This expression is formed by using the interjection **haydi** at the beginning of the action and the suffix -**(y)alim**/-**(y)elim** at the end of the verb. Here are some examples:
Haydi, lokantaya gidelim.   Let's go to the restaurant.
Haydi, (biz) katılalım.   Let's join in.
Haydi, yüzelim.   Let's swim.
Haydi, bir kayık kiralıyalım. Let's rent a boat.

CUMARTESI Akşamleyin SATURDAY

things to do

6.4 Read the two advertisements below and answer the following questions in Turkish. Questions 3 and 4 refer to the poster on the right.

1 What is being advertised here?
2 What kind of music will be played?
3 What time does the performance begin?
4 How much are the tickets?

Eşsiz bir
yemek ve müzik ziyafeti

Fasl-ı Konak

Geçmişin unutulmaz Fasıl gecelerini
bir Osmanlı vezirinin konağında yaşayın.
Musikimizin klasik, neo klasik en seçkin
eserlerini TRT sanatçıları Recep Birgit,
Galip Sokullu, Melihat Gülses, Tülay
Canik, Refi!. Akbulut ve Koray Safkan'dan
her hafta PAZARTESİ ve PERŞEMBE
geceleri dinleyerek nostaljiyi tadın.

REŞAT PAŞA KONAĞI
RESTAURANT
Tel: 361 34 11-361 34 87-361 35 89

İSTANBUL GECELERİ
★ ★ ★ ★ ★ ★ ★ ★ ★ ★ ★ ★ ★

CADDEBOSTAN
MAKSİM

SİBEL CAN

NAZAN SORAY
OSMAN Y.DERELİ
NİLÜFER ÖZ
DENİZ EREN
HALE DİKMEN

İBRAHİM TATLISES

SAMİ ÖZKANLI İdaresinde   ÇARŞAMBA BAYANLARA
MEYDAN FASLI   PAZAR UMUMA MATİNE
Saat: 20.30 da   -Yemekli   40.000
• Fiks Menü Servisimiz Vardır •

TALKING ABOUT YOURSELF

Meslekler/Occupations

Jill and Daniel are invited to a reception party given by their
Turkish friends Tarık and Neslihan.

Tarık:	*(to Jill)* Size arkadaşım Mehmet Akçapınar'ı tanıştırayım.
Mehmet:	Tanıştığımıza memnun oldum.
Tarık:	Daniel, eşim Neslihan ile tanıştınız sanıyorum.
Daniel:	Evet, Nasılsınız Neslihan Hanım?
Neslihan:	Teşekkürler. Jill Hanım siz nasılsınız?
Jill:	Teşekkürler, iyiyiz.
Neslihan:	İzniniz ile, diğer misafirler geliyorlar. Lütfen, kendi evinizde gibi hissediniz.
Mehmet:	*(to Daniel)* Affedersiniz, mesleğiniz nedir?
Daniel:	Ben bir elektronik mühendisiyim.
Tarık:	Çok iyi bir meslek. Modern yaşantıda elektronik çok şey kullanıyoruz.
Daniel:	Sizin mesleğiniz nedir?
Tarık:	Ben bir cerrahım. Eşim diş doktorudur.
Mehmet:	Ben de öğretmenim, bir okulun baş öğretmeniyim.
Tarık:	Jill Hanım, sizin mesleğiniz nedir?
Jill:	Ah, ben bir ev hanımıyım.
Mehmet:	Evet, sizin işiniz gerçekten çok yorucu! Ev işi, çocuklar, yemek, sonra biz erkekler!

What do you do?
For a list of professions see page 84.

Size arkadaşım ... tanıştırayım.	Let me introduce my friend to you.
Tanıştığımıza memnun oldum.	I am pleased to meet you.
Eşim ... ile tanıştınız sanıyorum	You have met my wife/husband ... I think
İzniniz ile ...	With your permission ...

Diğer misafirler geliyorlar.	Other guests are coming.
Kendi evinizde gibi hissediniz.	Please feel at home.
Sizin mesleğiniz nedir?	What is your occupation?
Ben bir mühendisim.	I am an engineer.
(Ben) koleje gidiyorum.	I go to high school.
Bir fabrikada çalışıyorum.	I work in a factory.
Bir bankada ...	in a bank
Bir hastanede ...	at a hospital
İşsizim.	I am unemployed.
Sizin işiniz gerçekten zor.	Your work is certainly hard.
çok iyi bir meslek	a very good occupation.
modern yaşantıda ...	in modern life ...
Elektronik çok şey kullanıyoruz.	We use a lot of electronic things.

cerrah	surgeon
Eşim diş doktorudur.	My wife is a dentist (*lit.* dental doctor).
ev işi çocuklar, yemek,	housework, children, food,
Sonra biz erkekler!	Then us men!

THE WEATHER

Hava durumu/Weather conditions

Daniel: **Bugün** hava gerçekten **çok sıcak**.
Mehmet: Evet, özellikle bu ay genel olarak hava sıcaktır.
Tarık: İngiltere'de hava nasıldır?
Jill: Genellikle yağmurlu ve kapalıdır.
Mehmet: İngiltere'de çok sis var. Hava nemlidir, doğru mu?
Daniel: Evet. Türkiye'de kışın soğuk olur mu?
Neslihan: Evet. Ege ve Akdeniz kıyıları dışında kış soğuktur. Fakat
            Türkiye'de dört mevsim yaşanır.
Jill: **Ben** sıcağı **tercih ederim**. Soğuk ve karlı havadan
            hoşlanmam.
Daniel: Ben rüzgarlı havayı sevmem.
Mehmet: Biz de güneşli ve açık, sıcak ve kuru havayı severiz.

What's the weather like?

Bugün çok sıcak.	It is very hot today.
gerçekten	in fact
özellikle	especially
genellikle/genel olarak	in general
Hava nasıl?	What is the weather like?
Hava sıcak/soğuk.	It is hot/cold.
güneşli/açık	sunny/clear
rüzgarlı/bulutlu, kapalı	windy/cloudy
yağmurlu/karlı	rainy/snowy
sisli/puslu	foggy
nemli/kuru	damp/dry
Yağmur yağıyor.	It is raining.
Kar yağıyor.	It is snowing.
Rüzgar esiyor.	The wind is blowing.
Fırtına çıkıyor.	The storm is coming.
Kışın soğuk olur mu?	Is it cold in winter?
ege ve Akdeniz kıyıları dışında	apart from the Aegean and Meditteranean coasts
Fakat Türkiye'de dört mevsim yaşanır.	But in Turkey four seasons are lived.
ben ... tercih ederim	I prefer
ben ... sevmem/hoşlanmam	I don't like

the way it works

How to say what you do

Ben bir mühendis**im**.   I'm an engineer.
     doktor**um**   a doctor
     müdür**üm**   a manager

This construction uses the verb **imek** (to be). It is a [noun + (imek)] structure.

But certain occupational words are made up from two or more nouns coupled together (e.g. electronics engineer). When this happens, you add a coupling suffix (elektronik mühendisi + im), which therefore needs a **y** as a liaison letter.
Ben bir banka müdürüy**üm**.   I'm a bank manager.

Two of these compound structures appeared in the dialogue:
Ben bir elektronik mühendisiy**im**.   I'm an electronics engineer.
Ben bir ev hanımıy**ım**.   I'm a housewife.

... and where you work

To say where you work use the locative case:

Ben bir fabrika**da** bir mühendisim.   I'm an engineer in a factory.
Ben bir çocuk hastahanesin**de** doktorum.   I'm a doctor in a children's hospital.

Talking about the weather

Hava nasıl? What's the weather like?
The answer may be constructed as follows:
Hava sıcaktır. It's hot.

The (**tir/dir**) part which means *is* (see Monday, page 5) can be omitted in conversation.

If you want to ask for a weather forecast, you need to use the simple future tense:
Hava nasıl **olacak?** What will the weather be like?
Hava soğuk **olacak.** It will be cold

To say "it is raining" one uses the present tense of **yağmak** + noun **yağmur** *(rain).*
Yağmur **yağıyor.**   It is raining.
Kar **yağıyor.**   It is snowing.

To say "it will rain" use the same construction with the future tense of **yağmak.**
Yağmur **yağacak.**   It will rain.
Kar **yağacak.**   It will snow.

things to do

7.1 Everyone in your party is talking about what they do. Can you join in?

Mark: an architect   Susan: an accountant

Charles: a businessman

Anna: a taxi driver   Bernard: a garbage collector   Helen: an artist

What do *you* do for a living?

71

7.2

HAVA DURUMU

| AÇIK | KARLI | KAPALI | YAĞMUR | SİSLİ |

İSTANBUL: Parçalı az bulutlu, -2°/6°
ANKARA: Parçalı bulutlu, -8°/4°
İZMİR: Az bulutlu, açık, -1°/11°
ADANA: Az bulutlu, açık, 7°/18°
ANTALYA: Az bulutlu, açık, 6°/16°
EDİRNE: Parçalı az bulutlu, -4°/9°
ESKİŞEHİR: Parçalı bulutlu, -8°/3°
İZMİT: Parçalı az bulutlu, -2°/8°
SAKARYA: Parçalı az bulutlu, -2°/8°
ZONGULDAK: Çok bulutlu, yağmurlu -9°/3°

AVRUPA'DA ÖNEMLİ MERKEZLER
LONDRA: Parçalı bulutlu, 8°
PARİS: Az bulutlu, 7°
ZÜRİH: Az bulutlu, 6°
CENEVRE: Az bulutlu, 15°
ROMA: Parçalı bulutlu, 14°
ATİNA: Az bulutlu, 14°

1 What's the weather like in İstanbul?
2 Is it raining in İzmir?
3 Is it snowing in the mountains?
4 Is it windy on the south coast?

72

TALKING ABOUT YOUR STAY

Görüsleriniz/Your observations

Daniel and Jill are talking to a Turkish tour guide, Nermin.

Jill: Biz burada kısa bir tatildeyiz.
Nermin: Kaç gün kalacaksınız?
Daniel: İki hafta.
Nermin: Daha önceden Türkiye'ye geldiniz mi?
Jill: Hayır, bu bizim ilk gelişimiz.
Nermin: Nerede kalıyorsunuz?
Daniel: Yusuf Otel'de kalıyoruz.
Nermin: Buradan hoşlandınız mı?
Jill: Evet, bize göre Türkiye çok değişik ve ilginç bir ülke.
Daniel: Bizce, Türkler çok konuksever insanlar. Türkiye'nin çok zengin bir tarihi ve kültürü var.

Have you enjoyed your stay?

Biz burada ...	We are here ...
... kısa bir tatildeyiz	... for a short vacation
... bir iş ziyaretinde	... on a business trip
... eski camileri incelemekte	... to study the old mosques
Kaç gün kalacaksınız?	How many days are you staying?
iki hafta/ay/yaklaşık iki gün	two weeks/months/about two days
Daha önceden Türkiye'ye geldiniz mi?	Have you been to Turkey before?
Mayıs ayının sonundan beri ...	... since the end of May
... buradayım	I've been here ...
Bu bizim ilk gelişimiz.	This is our first visit.
Nerede kalıyorsunuz?	Where are you staying?
Yusuf Otel'de kalıyoruz.	We are staying at the Hotel Yusuf.
Buradan hoşlandınız mı?	Have you enjoyed (lit. liked) it here?
Bize göre ... /Bana göre ...	In our view ... .In my view ...
... çok değişik ve ilginç	... very different and interesting
Türkler çok konuksever insanlar.	Turks are very hospitable people.
Türkiye'nin çok zengin bir tarihi ve kültürü var.	Turkey has a very rich history and culture.

TALKING ABOUT HOBBIES

Hobileriniz nelerdir?/What are your hobbies?

Cem, Esra, Jill, and Daniel are talking about their hobbies.

Cem: Ben açık hava sporlarını severim. Her hafta sonunda, bisikletle yakın köylere giderim. Pazartesi günleri golf oynarım. Cumartesi öğleden sonra atçılık kulübüne giderim.

Jill: Ben klasik müziği çok severim. Piyano ve kemanı iyi çalarım. Haftada bir defa konsere giderim. Salı günleri keman, cuma günleride piyano dersleri alırım.

Esra: Ben biraz sanatkarım. Resim çizerim ve sulu boya yaparım. Çarşamba akşamları çömlekçilik kursuna giderim. Şehirde bütün sergilere giderim.

Daniel: Ben macerayı severim. Dağcılık ve kayak yaparım. Yazın denizde dalgıçlık yaparım. Haftada iki günde uçuş okuluna giderim.

Sports and hobbies

For a list of sporting activities see page 84.

... severim	I like ...
Ben açık hava sporlarını severim.	I like outdoor sports.
hafta sonunda	on the weekend
her hafta sonunda	on weekends

bisikletle	by bicycle
yakın köylere	to nearby villages
her Pazartesi/Cumartesi	on Mondays/Saturdays
her Pazartesi sabahı/akşamı	on Monday mornings/evenings
Golf oynarım.	I play golf.
golf kulübü/atçılık kulübü	golf club/riding club
Ben piyano çalarım.	I play (the) piano.
keman/saz	violin/lute
günde bir defa	once a day
haftada iki defa	twice a week
Konsere giderim.	I go to a concert.
Piyano dersleri alırım.	I take piano lessons.
Ben biraz sanatkarım.	I am a bit of an artist.
Resim çizerim.	I draw.
ve sulu boya/yağlı boya yaparım	and do watercolors/oil painting
çömlekçilik kursu	pottery course
bütün sergiler	all exhibitions
Ben macerayı severim.	I like adventure.
Dağcılık yaparım.	I go mountaineering.
kayak/dalgıçlık/uçuş	skiing/scuba diving/flying

the way it works

How many times, how often

In order to express this concept, use **defa** or **kere** together with the number of occurrences or happenings.

bir **defa** *or* bir **kere**   once
iki **defa** *or* iki **kere**   twice
üç **defa** *or* üç **kere**   three times

If these are used with a period of time they may appear as such:
haftada bir **defa** *or* haftada bir **kere**:   once a week
yılda iki **defa**   *or* yılda iki **kere**:   twice a year

If the events take place regularly:
her pazartesi or pazartesi günleri: every Monday
her hafta: every week
her hafta salı günleri: every week on Tuesday
her hafta Salı günü akşamları: every week on Tuesday evenings

The aorist tense: a reminder

The aorist tense is frequently used in promises, requests, stage directions, vivid present cases, and also in expressing a continuing activity or habit, as in this unit:
Ben piyano çala**rım**.   I play (the) piano.
Cumartesi atçılık kulübüne gide**rim**. On Saturdays I go to the riding club.

things to do

7.3   See if you can fill out this form giving details about yourself in Turkish:

```
Ad: ....................................................................
Soyadı: ..............................................................
Doğum tarihi: ....................................................
Doğum yeri: ........................................................
Medeni Durum: ..................................................
Meslek: ..............................................................
İş yeri: ...............................................................
Hobiler: .............................................................
Sevilen spor dalları: ...........................................
Sevilen müzik: ...................................................
Sevilen sanat dalları: .........................................
Sevilen renkler: .................................................
Sevilen ülkeler: .................................................
```

7.4   At their job interviews two people are asked about their hobbies.

A   You are Alison. Give the interviewer the following information:
1   You like classical music.
2   You play the violin and the piano.
3   You go to a concert about once a week.
4   On Monday evenings you go to a music club.

B   You are George. Give the interviewer the following information:
1   You are an artist.
2   You like drawing and doing watercolors.
3   You attend a pottery course on Thursday mornings.
4   You go to all the exhibitions.

KEY TO EXERCISES

1.1 Merhaba Bay Oğuzkan. Hoşça kalınız Bay Oğuzkan. 2 Merhaba Engin Bey. Hoşça kalınız Engin Bey. 3 Merhaba Bayan Köylü. Hoşça kalınız Bayan Köylü. 4 Merhaba Bayan Yarımcı. Hoşça kalınız Bayan Yarımcı.
1.2 1 Merhaba. Nasılsınız? 2 Günaydın. 3 İyi akşamlar. Tanıştığımıza memnun oldum. 4 İyi günler. Nasılsınız?
1.3 You: Merhaba, Oğuz Bey.
You: Çok teşekkür ederim, iyiyim. Ya siz?
You: Tanıştığımıza memnun oldum. Nasılsınız?
1.4 You: İyi akşamlar. Boş odanız var mı?
You: Bir hafta için.
You: Ben tek kişilik duşlu bir oda istiyorum.
You: Peki. Odada duş var mı?
You: Peki. Ücreti ne kadar?
1.5 Bira, kırmızı şarap, meyva suyu, maden suyu, çay.

2.1 Frances için, ekmek, beyaz peynir ve bir Türk kahvesi getiriniz. Peter için, ekmek, tereyağı ve reçel getiriniz lütfen. Andrew için, ekmek, zeytin ve meyva suyu getiriniz lütfen. Jane için, ekmek, reçel ve bir Türk kahvesi getiriniz, lütfen.
2.2 1 Dört kişilik bir masanız var mı? 2 Lütfen listeyi getiriniz. 3 İçecek neler var? 4 Ben, bir, çorba, bir şiş kebap, bir Adana kebap ve bir karışık salata istiyorum. 5 Bir şişe rakı lütfen. 6 Hesabı getirir misiniz?
2.3 You: Bir kilo üzüm istiyorum, lütfen.
You: Şeftaliler kaç lira?
You: Bir kilo istiyorum, lütfen.
You: Yarım kilo domates lütfen.
You: Hayır. Hepsi bu kadar. Ne kadar?
2.4 200 grams of feta cheese
    a loaf of bread
    1 liter of milk
    1 package of tea
    ½ kilo of rice
    250 grams of olives.
2.5 1 Küçük mavi bir kilim [satın almak istiyorum] 2 Bir semaver 3 Büyük bir seramik tabak 4 Bir kaç tesbih taşı 5 Beyaz bir gömlek.

3.1 1 Affedersiniz, postahane nerededir? 2 Turist Danışma

bürosu nerededir? 3 Osman Paşa Caddesi nerededir? 4 İstasyon (gar) nerededir?
3.2 1 Kaleye nasıl gidebiliriz? (gidebilirim) or Kaleye nasıl giderim? 2 Limana nasıl gidebilirim? 3 Müzeye nasıl gidebilirim? 4 Camiye nasıl gidebilirim?
3.3 1 Go straight along this road, then take the first street on the (turn) right. The mosque is there. 2 Go straight along this road. [Take] the first street on the left. The post office is there, on the corner. 3 Go straight along this road. The station is at the end of the road, on the right.
3.4 You: Hitit Müzesine gitmek istiyorum. Buradan oraya nasıl gidebilirim (or giderim)?
You: Dolmuş durağı nerededir?
You: Dolmuş bizi oraya dosdoğru götürecek mi?
You: Çok teşekkürler.
3.5 (a) Efes'e/İzmir'e/Bodrum'a/Kuşadası'na otobüs ne zaman hareket ediyor? or Efes'e/İzmir'e/Bodrum'a/Kuşadası'na otobüs be zaman kalkıyor? (b) Saat dokuzu on geçe. Saat dokuz buçukta. Saat on da. Saat onu kırk geçe (or Saat onbire yirmi kala). (c) Efes'e otobüs ne zaman varacak? İzmir'e otobüs ne zaman varacak? Bodrum'a otobüs ne zaman varacak? Kuşadası'na otobüs ne zaman varacak?
3.6 You: Kuşadası'na gitmek istiyorum.
You: Bu sabah.
You: İki kişi için.
You: Bir bilet ne kadar?
You: Lütfen iki gidiş bileti.
You: Adım _____ .
You: İşte 15,000 lira, teşekkürler.

4.1 You: Ben biraz Amerikan doları banknotu değiştirmek istiyorum.
You: Yüz dolar. Bugün döviz kuru nedir?
You: Teşekkürler.
4.2 Benim pasaportum. Benim seyahat çeklerim. Benim kredi kartım. Benim İstanbul'a tren biletim. Benim Türk paralarım.
4.3 You: İyi günler, efendim. İngiltere'ye iki kartpostal pulu, lütfen.
You: Teşekkürler. Amerika'ya dört

mektup pulu lütfen.
You: Evet, tamam. Hepsi ne kadar?
You: İşte paranız. Affedersiniz,
Londra'ya telefon edebilir miyim?
You: Çok teşekkürler, hoşça kalınız.
4.4 1 Posta pulu satın almalıyım. 2
Avusturalya'ya bir paket
göndermeliyim. 3 Bankaya gitmeliyim.
4 Biraz seyahat çeki bozdurmalıyım. 5
Otobüs terminaline gitmeliyim. 6
İzmir'e bir bilet satın almalıyım.

5.1 Biz küçük bir araba istiyoruz. 2 Üç
gün için kaç lira? 3 Depozito ödemeli
miyim? 4 Biz, Peugeot'u istiyoruz. Lütfen
anahtarı veriniz. 5 Arabayı Antalya'da
bırakabilir miyiz? (teslim
edebilirmiyiz?)
5.2 Lütfen 30 litrelik süper benzin
veriniz. 2 Lütfen lastiklerin havasına bir
bakınız. 3 Tamir yapıyor musunuz (or
onarabilir misiniz?) 4 Bir kayış satın
almak istiyorum. 5 Lütfen fatura veriniz.
5.3 Trafik polisi, oto tamircisi, garaj
5.4 1 Affedersiniz, garaj nerededir? 2
Arabamız bozuldu. 3 Benzinimiz
tükendi. 4 Bir bakar mısınız?
5.5 You: İshal için bir şeyiniz var mı?
You: Peki, tamam. Günde kaç tane
almalıyım?
You: Teşekkürler. Kaç lira?
5.6 Kate: Güneşte yandım. David:
Midem ağrıyor. Peter: Ayak - bileğim
burkuldu. Maggie: Kolumu yaktım. You:
Ben de, plajda düştüm ve dizimi
incittim.
5.7 1 Pasaportumu kaybettim. 2
Anahtarımı kaybettim. 3 El çantamı
kaybettim. 4 Fotoğraf makinemi
kaybettim. 5 Biletimi kaybettim.

6.1 1 Ben tenis oynamasını severim. 2
Ben futbol seyretmesini severim. 3 Ben
yelkenciliği severim. 4 Ben kayak
yapmayı severim. 5 Ben golf
oynamasını severim. 6 Ben ata binmeyi
severim. 7 Ben yüzmeyi severim. 8 Ben
yürümeyi severim.
6.2 Biz tenis oynamak istiyoruz. Boş bir
tenis sahası var mı?
Bu sabah, saat onbir gibi olabilir.
Tamam, Bir kaç tenis topu kiralamak
istiyorum.
6.3 1 Stadyum nerededir?

2 Yüzme havuzu nerededir? 3 Su
kayağı yarışması nerededir? 4
Basketbol turnuvası nerededir?
6.4 Fasl-ı Konak

1 Yemek ve Türk Sanat Müzik
  Programı.
2 Türk Sanat ve Hafif Müziği
3 Her hafta pazartesi ve perşembe
  geceleri.
4 Bir kişi için otuz beş bin lira (35,000
  T.L.).

İstanbul Geceleri
1 İstanbul'da yemekli bir Türk Müzik
  Gecesi
2 Türk sanat, halk ve hafif müzikleri.
3 Her akşam, saat 20.30 da.
4 Yemekli kırk bin lira (40,000 T.L.)

7.1 Mark: Ben bir mimarım. Susan: Ben
bir muhasebeciyim. Charles: Ben bir iş
adamıyım. Anna: Ben bir taksi
şöförüyüm. Bernard: Ben bir
çöpçüyüm. Helen: Ben bir artistim.
Mesleğiniz nedir?
7.2 İstanbul'da hava nasıl? 2 İzmir'de
yağmur yağıyor mu? 3 Dağlar da kar
yağmıyor? 4 Güney kıyıları rüzgarlı değil.
7.3 1 Name 2 Last name 3 Date of birth
4 Place of birth 5 Marital Status 6
Occupation 7 Workplace 8 Hobbies 9
Preferred sports 10 Preferred music 11
Preferred branches of art 12 Preferred
colors 13 Preferred countries
7.4 A 1 Ben, klasik müziği severim. 2
Ben, keman ve piyano çalarım. 3 Ben,
haftada bir defa konsere giderim. 4
Ben, pazartesi akşamları bir müzik
kulübüne giderim. B 1 Ben, bir
sanatkarım. 2 Resim çizerim ve sulu
boya yaparım. 3 Ben, perşembe
sabahları çömlekçilik kursuna giderim.
4 Ben, bütün sergilere giderim.

VOCABULARY

English-Turkish topic vocabularies

Numbers

1	bir	19	ondokuz	70	yetmiş		
2	iki	20	yirmi	80	seksen		
3	üç	21	yirmibir	90	doksan		
4	dört	22	yirmiiki	100	yüz		
5	beş	23	yirmiüç	200	ikiyüz		
6	altı	24	yirmidört	900	dokuzyüz		
7	yedi	25	yirmibeş	1000	bin		
8	sekiz	26	yirmialtı	8000	sekizbin		
9	dokuz	27	yirmiyedi				
10	on	28	yirmisekiz				
11	onbir	29	yirmidokuz	first	birinci		
12	oniki	30	otuz	second	ikinci		
13	onüç	31	otuzbir	third	üçüncü		
14	ondört	32	otuziki	fourth	dördüncü		
15	onbeş		etc	fifth	beşinci		
16	onaltı	40	kırk	ninth	dokuzuncu		
17	onyedi	50	elli	tenth	onuncu		
18	onsekiz	60	altmış				

Months

January	Ocak	July	Temmuz
February	Şubat	August	Ağustos
March	Mart	September	Eylül
April	Nisan	October	Ekim
May	Mayıs	November	Kasım
June	Haziran	December	Aralık

Seasons

Spring	İlkbahar
Summer	Yaz
Autumn	Sonbahar
Winter	Kış

Clothes

belt	kayış	pajamas	pijama
blouse	gömlek	pants	pantalon
bra	sütyen	purse	el çantası
coat	palto-manto	raincoat	yağmurluk
dress	elbise	scarf	eşarp
gloves	eldiven	shirt	gömlek
hat	şapka	skirt	etek
jacket	ceket	socks	çoraplar
jeans	blujin	stockings	kadın çorabı
nightgown	gecelik	suit	takım elbise
overalls	iş elbisesi	underpants	kilot

Colors

black	siyah, kara	pink	pembe	light	açık
blue	mavi	red	kırmızı	dark blue	koyu mavi
brown	kahverengi	white	beyaz	light grey	açık gri
green	yeşil	yellow	sarı		
gray	gri	dark	koyu		

VOCABULARY

Materials

cotton	**pamuk**	silk	**ipek**	velvet	**kadife**
leather	**deri**	silken	**ipekli**	wool	**yün**
nylon	**naylon**	suede	**süet**	woollen	**yünlü**

At the pharmacy

adhesive bandage	**yara bandı**	night-duty	**nöbetci eczane**
antiseptic	**antiseptik**	pharmacy	
bandage	**sargı bezi**	ointment	**merhem**
cotton	**pamuk**	painkiller	**ağrı kesici**
cough drops	**boğaz yumaşatıcı**	prescription	**reçete**
cough syrup	**öksürük şurubu**	sleeping pills	**uyku hapı**
medicine	**ilaç**	thermometer	**termometre**

Toiletries

baby food	**bebek maması**	razor	**jilet**
brush	**fırça**	safety pin	**çengelli iğne**
comb	**tarak**	shampoo	**şampuan**
cream	**krem**	soap	**sabun**
deodorant	**deodorant**	suntan lotion	**güneş yağı**
electric razor	**elektrikli traş**	tissues	**kağıt mendil**
	makinesi	toothpaste	**diş macunu**
perfume	**parfüm**	toothbrush	**diş fırçası**

Food

Menu (general words)

appetizers	**mezeler**	fish dishes	**balık yemekleri**
barbecued	**meşe kömürde**	fried	**kızartma**
	ızgara	fruits	**meyvalar**
boiled	**haşlama**	grilled	**ızgarada**
desserts	**tatlılar**	in a casserole	**güveçte**
dishes with meat	**etli yemekler**	soups	**çorbalar**
dishes with olive oil	**zeytinyağlı**	vegetables	**sebzeler**
	yemekleri		

Appetizers

carrot salad	**havuç salatası**	fried mussels	**midye tava**
chicken circassian	**çerkez tavuğu**	mixed salad	**karışık salata**
cucumber in yogurt	**cacık**	pinto bean dish	**barbunya**
dry red beans dish	**pilaki**		**pilaki**
eggplant salad	**patlıcan**	shepherd's salad	**çoban salatası**
	salatası	stuffed mussels	**midye dolması**
fried eggplants	**patlıcan**		
	kızartması		
pepper	**biber . . .**		
zucchini	**kabak . . .**		

VOCABULARY

Soups

flour soup	**un çorbası**	tripe soup	**işkembe çorbası**
red lentil soup	**kırmızı mercimek çorbası**	vegetable soup	**sebze çorbası**
		wedding soup	**düğün çorbası**
semolina soup	**irmik çorbası**	yogurt soup	**yayla çorbası**

Some fish dishes

fillets of sole	**dil filetosu**
grey mullet with vegetables	**kefal pilakisi**
mackerel in sauce	**salçalı uskumru**
salt-cured tuna	**lakerda**
sea bass in white wine	**beyaz şarap soslu levrek**
skewered shrimp	**karides şiş**
steamed anchovies	**hamsi buğulama**
swordfish	**kılıç**
turbot	**kalkan**

Some meat dishes

forest kebab	**orman kebabı**	meatballs, dry	**kuru köfte**
gardener's kebab	**bahçevan kebabı**	meatballs, in tomato	**İzmir köftesi**
		shish kebab	**şiş kebabı**
hunter's kebab	**avcı kebabı**	sultan's delight	**hünkar beğendi**
kebab casserole	**güveç kebabı**	woman's casserole	**hanım güveci**
kebab with yogurt	**yoğurtlu kebap**		
meat balls, chicken	**tavuk köftesi**		

Poultry

chicken with rice	**tavuklu pilar**
cream chicken	**kremalı piliç**
duck with mushrooms	**mantarlı ördek**
roasted chicken	**fırında piliç kızartması**

Vegetable dishes

broad beans in oil	**zeytinyağlı bakla**
fresh green bean dish	**taze fasulye**
fried potatoes	**patates kızartması**
green pea dish	**taze bezelye**
leek with rice	**zeytinyağlı pırasa**
mixed vegetable dish	**türlü**
mousakka	**patlıcan musakka**
potato dish	**etli patates**
stuffed vegetables	**dolma**
eggplant	**patlıcan dolması**
peppers	**biber dolması**
tomatoes	**domates dolması**
vine leaves	**yaprak dolması**
zucchini	**kabak dolması**

(Hot dolmas are with meat, cold dolmas are appetizers.)

VOCABULARY

Pastries

Cigarette pastry with cheese	**peynirli sigara böreği**
pastry with meat	**kıymalı börek**
with cheese	**peynirli börek**
with spinach	**ıspanaklı börek**
pizza with cheese	**peynirli pide**
with meat	**kıymalı pide**
with egg	**yumurtalı pide**
with Turkish salami	**sucuklu pide**
water pastry with cheese	**peynirli su böreği**
with meat	**kıymalı su böreği**

Desserts

baklava	**baklava**	ladies' navel	**hanım göbeği**
beauty's lips	**dilber dudağı**	milk pudding	**muhallebi**
cake in syrup	**revani**	semolina helva	**irmik helvası**
chicken breasts	**tavuk göğsü**	vanilla pudding	**keşkül**
kadaif	**kadayıf**		

Fruit

apples	**elma**	peaches	**şeftali**
apricots	**kayısı**	pears	**armut**
banana	**muz**	plum	**erik**
cherry	**vişne**	pomegranate	**nar**
figs	**incir**	quince	**ayva**
grapes	**üzüm**	strawberry	**çilek**
lemon	**limon**	sweet melons	**kavun**
mulberries	**dut**	watermelons	**karpuz**
orange	**portakal**		

Groceries

bread	**ekmek**	margarine	**sana yağı**
cheese	**peynir**	milk	**süt**
coffee	**kahve**	oil	**likit yağ**
cookies	**bisküvit**	pasta	**makarna**
eggs	**yumurta**	rice	**pirinç**
flour	**un**	sugar	**şeker**
jam	**reçel**	tea	**çay**

Parts of the body

ankle	**ayak bileği**	finger	**parmak**	lip	**dudak**
arm	**kol**	foot	**ayak**	mouth	**ağız**
back	**sırt**	hair	**saç**	neck	**boyun**
chest	**göğüs**	hand	**el**	shoulder	**omuz**
ear	**kulak**	head	**baş**	skin	**deri**
elbow	**dirsek**	heart	**kalp**	stomach	**karın, mide**
eye	**göz**	hip	**kalça**	throat	**boğaz**
eyes	**gözler**	knee	**diz**	tooth	**diş**
face	**yüz**	leg	**bacak**		

VOCABULARY

Sports

basketball	**basketbol**	sailing	**yelkencilik**
billiards	**bilardo**	scuba diving	**dalgıçlık**
chess	**satranç**	shooting	**atıcılık**
climbing	**tırmanış**	skiing	**kayak**
fishing	**balık avlama**	soccer	**futbol**
flying	**uçuş**	swimming	**yüzme**
golf	**golf**	tennis	**tenis**
horse racing	**binicilik, atçılık**	volleyball	**voleybol**
jogging	**koşma**		

Parts of the car

battery	**akü**	headlights	**uzun fenerler/farlar**
brakes	**frenler**	ignition	**marş anahtarı**
bulbs	**ampüller**	radiator	**radyatör**
clutch	**debriyaj**	spark plugs	**bujiler**
distributor	**distribütör**	steering wheel	**direksiyon**
engine	**motor**	tires	**araba lastikleri**
exhaust	**egzos**	turn signal	**sinyal lambası**
fan belt	**motor kayışı**	wheels	**tekerlekler**
gas tank	**benzin tankı**	windshield	**araba ön camı**
gears	**vitesler**	wipers	**cam silecekleri**

Professions

accountant	**muhasebeci**
attorney	**avukat, noter**
architect	**mimar**
bank teller	**banka memuru**
banker	**bankacı, banker**
builder	**inşaatcı**
businessman	**iş adamı**
businesswoman	**iş hanımı**
chef	**ahçıbaşı, şef**
civil servant	**devlet memuru**
company director	**firma direktörü**
computer programmer	**kompüter programlayıcısı**
computer operator	**kompüter operatörü**
dentist	**dişçi, diş doktoru**
doctor	**hekim, tabib, doktor**
engineer	**mühendis**
(civil)	**inşaat mühendisi**
(chemical)	**kimya mühendisi**
(electronic)	**elektronik mühendisi**
hairdresser	**kadın berberi**
housewife	**ev hanımı**
interpreter	**tercüman**
journalist	**gazeteci**
mechanic	**araba tamircisi, ustası**
nurse	**hemşire, hasta bakıcı**
pharmacist	**eczacı, kimyager**

policeman	**polis**
real estate agent	**emlakçı**
salesman	**satış elemanı**
secretary	**sekreter**
student	**öğrenci**
teacher	**öğretmen**

Workplaces

bank	**banka**	garage	**garaj**
clinic	**klinik**	hospital	**hastahane**
college	**üniversite**	laboratory	**laboratuvar**
factory	**fabrika**	office	**ofis**
firm	**firma**	shop	**dükkan**

Turkish-English vocabulary

acaba I wonder if

acele hurry, urgent, hurried action, at once

acı pain, ache, hot (pepper, etc.)

acil hastahanesi emergency hospital

aç hungry

açık open

ad name

adet (or tane) a single item

adres address

aferin (or aferim) bravo, well done

affetmek to excuse (person)

affedersiniz I beg your pardon; excuse me

afiyet health

afiyetle with a good appetite

afiyet olsun bon appetit

ağrımak to ache, hurt, to suffer pain

ağrı kesici painkiller

ağrıyan aching, hurting

aile family

Akdeniz the Mediterranean

akşam evening

alerji allergy

alet tool, implement

alıcı customer, receiver

alış-veriş shopping

almak to take

alınmak to be taken

ambülans ambulance

ana (or anne) mother

anahtar key

anlamak to understand, to comprehend

araba car, automobile

aramak to search, to look for

arasıra now and then, from time to time, occasionally

arka back, back side, rear

arkadaş friend, fellow

artist actor, actress

arzu wish, want, request

arzu etmek to wish for, to long for, to desire

astım (astımlı) asthma (asthma sufferer)

aşağı down, downwards

aşağıda below, downstairs

at horse

atçılık horseback riding, horses

Avrupa Europe

ay month, moon

ayırtmak to have reserved

ayrılmak to part, to leave

az few, not much, little

baba father

bagaj luggage

bahçe garden, park

bakmak to look (at), to pay attention to

balık fish

balkon balcony

balkonlu with balcony

bana to me

banka bank

banka kartı bank card

banknot banknote, bill

banyo bath, bathroom

banyolu with bath

bar bar

bardak cup, mug, glass

basketbol basketball

baş head, start, beginning

başka other, another, different

başlamak to begin, to start

bavul suitcase

bazen sometimes

belediye otobüsü public bus

belki perhaps, maybe

ben I

benim mine

benzin gas

benzinci gas station

beyan declaration

beyaz peynir feta cheese

VOCABULARY

bıçak knife
biber pepper
bilet ticket
bilmek to know
bira beer
biraz a little, some
birinci the first
birkaç a few, some
bisiklet bicycle
bizce according to us, in our opinion
bizim our, ours
boğaz olmak to have a sore throat
boş empty, vacant, free
bozdurmak to change money
bozuk broken, out of order
bozuk para small change, coins
bozulmak to become out of order, to break down
bölge region, district
böyle like this
bu this
bunlar these
buçuk and a half
bugün today
bulanmak (mide) to be upset (stomach)
bulut cloud
bulutlu cloudy
bura this place, here
burada in this place, here
burkmak or burkulmak to sprain (a joint), to twist
burkulma twisting, twist
buyurun or buyurunuz please come in; help yourself, here it is, take it, welcome
büfe buffet
büro office
bütün whole, entire, total, complete
büyük great, large, big, elder

cadde main road in a city

cami mosque
can soul, life
ceket jacket
cerrah surgeon
cümbüş kind of mandolin with metal body
çabucak quickly
çabuk quick, fast, quickly
çağırmak to call, to invite
çalgı (or çalgı aleti) musical instrument
çalmak to play a musical instrument
çalınmak to be stolen
çalışmak to work, to study, to try
çanta bag, case
çarşı market
çatal fork
çay tea
çek check
çek kartı check card
çektirmek to have (it) taken
çeşit kind, sort, variety
çevirmek to turn, to change (into), to dial (a telephone)
çeyrek a quarter
çıkış exit
çıkmak to exit
çift couple, pair, double
çoban shepherd
çocuk child, infant
çocuk bahçesi children's playground
çok much, a lot
çömlek earthenware pot
çömlekçlik pottery

da (de, ta, te) too, also
dan beri (den beri etc) since
dağ mountain
dağcı mountaineer
dağcılık mountaineering
daha more, further
dahil including
dakika minute
dal branch
danışma information office

dans dance
dans etmek to dance
dansöz dancer (f)
darbuka small drum
davet invitation
davul large drum
defa (or kere) time, turn, again
değerli valuable, worth
değil not
değişik different
değiştirmek to exchange (for), to change
deniz sea
depozito deposit, security
derhal at once, immediately
ders lesson
dış outside, exterior
dışında outside of
dışarı outdoors
dışarıda outside
diğer the other, next
dikkat be careful, look out!
dilim slice, strip
dişçi (or diş doktoru) dentist
diyabetik diabetic
doğan falcon, hawk
doğru right, correct, straight, direct
doğum birth
doğum evi or hastahanesi maternity hospital
doğum kontrol hapı (birth control) pill
doğum tarihi birthdate
doğum yeri place of birth
doktor doctor
doldurmak to fill in
dolmuş shared taxi
dolmuşçu dolmuş driver
dolu full, hailstones
dosdoğru straight ahead
dönmek to turn around, to go around
dörtyol intersection
döviz foreign exchange
döviz kuru foreign exchange rates
durak stop (bus, dolmuş)

VOCABULARY

duş shower
duşlu with shower
düğme button, switch
dükkan shop
dün yesterday
düşmek to fall
düşünmek to think

eczacı pharmacist
eczane pharmacy, drugstore
eğlence entertainment
ehliyet driver's license
ekip team, company
ekmek bread
elde dokunmuş handwoven
elçilik embassy
elektronik electronic
elektrik electrical
elma apple
el sanatı handicrafts
en most
enformasyon (or **informasyon**) information
erkek man, male
erken (or **erkenden**) early
ertesi the next, the following (day, week etc.)
eski old
eskitmek to wear out, to use up
eş partner, husband or wife
eşya things, objects, furniture
etyemez vegetarian
ev house
ev hanımı housewife
evet yes
evvel before, earlier
evvelki gün the day before

fabrika firm, company, manufacturing company
fakat but
fatura receipt, bill
fazla excess, more
feribot ferry boat
fırtına storm, gale

fiş coupon, form
fiyat price
folklör folk
fotoğraf photography, photograph
fotoğraf makinesi camera

gar train station
garson waiter
gaz gas (accelerator in car)
gazete newspaper
gece night
gecelik for a night
geç late, delayed
geçen hafta last week
geçmek to pass
geçmiş olsun get well soon
gelmek to come (from, to), to arrive
genel general
genellikle (or **genel olarak**) in general
gerçek real, true, genuine
gerçekten in fact, actually, really
gerekmek to be necessary, needed, required
geri back, backward, behind
getirmek to fetch, to bring
gibi like
gidiş departure, going
gidiş–geliş or **gidiş-dönüş** round-trip (ticket)
gişe memuru ticket vendor
gitar guitar
gitmek to go, to leave, to depart
golf golf
göndermek to send, to dispatch
gönderen sender
görmek to see
göre (-(e) göre) according to, in respect of
görülmek to be seen

görüş seeing, opinion, observation
görüşmek to meet, to see each other
götürmek to take away, to carry off
gül rose
güle güle good-bye
gümrük custom, duty, tariff
gün day
güneş – güneşli sun, sunny
güneş yanığı sunburn
günlük (or **gün başına**) per day, daily
gürültü noise
güzel beautiful, pretty, nice

hafif light
hafif müzik Turkish pop music
hafta week
hakiki genuine, true, real
halk folk, people, nation
halk müziği folk music
hamile pregnant
hangi which
hap pill, medicine, tablet
harabe ruins
hareket departure
hareket etmek to start, to set out on, to move
harita map
hasta sick, ill, unwell, patient
hasta bakıcı nurse
hastahane hospital
hata mistake, error, fault
hava air, atmosphere, weather
hava basmak to put air into something
hava durumu weather situation
hava raporu weather report
hava alanı airport
havlu towel
havuz pool, pond
hayat life

haydi (or hadi!) come on

hayır no

hazımsızlık indigestion

hazır ready, prepared

hazır olmak to be ready

hediye gift, present

hemen at once, right now

hemen hemen almost, very nearly

hemşire nurse

henüz only now, yet, still

hepsi all of it

hepsi bu kadar that is all!

her every, each

hesap bill, account

hissetmek to feel

hobi hobby

hoş pleasant, agreeable

hoş bulduk I am pleased to see you, thank you (in response to **hoş geldiniz.**)

hoş geldiniz welcome

hoşa gitmek or **hoşuna gitmek** to please, to be agreeable to

hoşlanmak to like, to be pleased with, to enjoy

içmek to drink, to smoke

içecek drink, beverage, drinkable

içeri inside

içeride inside, within

içerik contents

için for, in order to

içinde within, in

içki alcoholic drink

iğne needle, pin, injection

iğne yapmak to give an injection

ilaç medicine, drug

ile with

ileri further on, forward, front

ilginç interesting

ılık tepid, lukewarm

ilk yardım first aid

imdat Help!

imek to be

imza signature

imzalamak to sign

incelemek to examine carefully

incinmek to be sprained, to be injured

incitmek to hurt, to injure, to sprain

insan man, human being

inşallah God willing, if God wills, I hope so

ipek silk, silken

iplik thread, yarn, fiber

ishal diarrhea

ishal olmak to have diarrhea

isim name, title

istasyon station, railway station, stop

istemek to want, to require, to need

iş work, business, occupation

iş adamı businessman

ışık light

iş yeri workplace

işsiz unemployed

işte here, thus, oh well, like that

itfaiye fire department

iyi good, well, in good health

izin permission, leave, permit

jiklet chewing gum

kabul etmek to accept, to agree, to approve

kaç how many? how much?

kaça what is the price?

kadar as much as, as many as, as . . . as

kağıt paper

kahvaltı breakfast

kahve coffee

kahvehane coffee shop, café

kalmak to remain, to stay, to stop

kalabalık crowded

kale castle, fortress

kalkmak to set out on a journey, to start

kambiyo foreign exchange

kambiyo memuru bank clerk for foreign transactions

kamyon truck

kanun a zither-like musical string instrument

kapalı shut, closed, overcast

kar snow

karlı snowy

kar yağmak to snow

karakol police station

karavan camper

karışık mixed, complex

karşı opposite, opposite side or direction

karşılaşmak to meet one another

karşılık return, equivalent

kartpostal postcard

kaset çalar tape player, cassette player

kaşık spoon

kat floor, stage

katılmak to join in, to participate

katip clerk

kayak (kayak yapmak) ski (to ski)

kaybetmek to lose

kaybolmak to be lost

kayık boat, rowboat

kayıp loss

kayıp eşya ofisi lost and found

kayış belt, strap

kaza accident, mishap

keman violin

kendi oneself

kendim myself

kırmak to break, to injure

kırık broken

kırılmak to be broken

kısa short

kış winter

kışın in winter

kıyı short, coast, edge

kız girl, daughter

kilim flat, woven rug

kilo kilogram

kilosu per kilogram

VOCABULARY

kilo vermek or **kilo kaybetmek** or **kilo atmak**   to lose weight
kilometre   kilometer
kilometre başına   per kilometer
kiralamak   to rent
kiralık   for rent
kirli   dirty, unclean
kişi   person, individual
kişilik   for (so many) persons
klasik   classical
klasik müzik   classical music
kod   code
kolay   easy
kolayca/kolaylıkla   easily
kolej   a kind of grammar school
komple   complete
vilayet konağı   town hall
konser   concert
kontrol   checking
kontrol etmek   to check
konuksever   hospitable
konuşma   conversation, dialogue
konuşmak   to talk, to chat, to speak
kopuk   broken apart, torn away
korkmak   to be afraid, to fear
koşmak   to run
köpek   dog
köşe   corner
köşebaşı   street corner, the corner
köy   village
köylü   villager
kredi   credit
kredi kartı   credit card
kullanmak   to use
kullanılmak   to be used
kulüp   club
kurs   course (of lessons, etc.)
kuru   dry, dried
kutu   small box or case
küçük   small, little, young

kültablası   ashtray
kültür   culture

lastik   tire, rubber
lazım   necessary
lazım olmak   to be necessary
leziz   delicious, tasty
liman   harbor, seaport
liste   list, menu
lokanta   restaurant
lütfen   please

macera   adventure
maden suyu   mineral water
mağaza   large store, shop
masa   table
medeni durum   marital status
mektup   letter
memnun   pleased, happy
memnun olmak   to be pleased, to be happy
memur   official, civil servant, officer
merak etmek   to be anxious about someone or something
merak etmeyiniz   please, don't worry
merdiven   steps, stairs
merkez   center
meslek   occupation, profession, career
metre   meter
mevsim   season
meyva   fruit
meyva suyu   fruit juice
milliyet   nationality
misafir   guest, visitor
modern   modern
motel   motel
motifli   patterned
motorsiklet   motorcycle
müdür   director, manager
müze   museum

nakit para   cash, ready money
nasıl   how
nasılsınız?   how are you?

ne   what, how (with adjectives), which
neden   why
nefes   breath, breathing
nefes almak   to breathe, to take a breath
nefis   excellent, exquisite
ne kadar   how much
ne kadar süre (or zaman)   how long (time)
nemli   moist, damp
nere   where
nerede   (in, at, on) where
nereden/nereli   from where
nerelisiniz?   where are you from?
nereye   where to
ne zaman   when
nezle   a cold
nezle olmak   to catch a cold
niçin   why? what for?
normal   normal
nöbetçi eczane   pharmacist on night duty
numara   number
numaralı   numbered

o   that, he, she, it
oda   room
ofis   office
oğul   son
okumak   to read
okul   school
okunmak   to be read
olmak   to be, to happen, to occur, to become
onarmak   to repair
onlar   those, they
onların   their, theirs
onun   his, her, hers, its, of him, her
ora   that place, there
orada   there
oradan   from there
oraya   to there
otel   hotel
oto   car
otobüs   bus
otopark   parking lot
otobüs terminali   bus station, coach terminal

VOCABULARY

oynamak to play, to play a
   game/a sport
oyun game, play, dance
o zaman then

ödemek to pay
öğlende, öğleyin at noon
öğleden sonra in the
   afternoon
öğrenmek to learn
öğretmen teacher
ön front
önde in the front
önden from the front
öne to the front
önünde in front of
önce (-den önce) before,
   first, at first
önemli important
örnek example,
   specimen, sample
özel personal, private,
   special
özellikle specially,
   particularly
özür dilemek to ask
   pardon, to beg to be
   excused

pahalı expensive
paket parcel, package
palto overcoat
pamuk cotton
pamuk ipliği cotton
   thread, cotton yarn
pansiyon boarding house,
   room
para money
para çekmek to withdraw
   (money from bank)
para yatırmak to deposit,
   to invest money in bank
parça small, piece
park park, garden, park
park etmek (or yapmak)
   to park (a car etc.)
pasaport passport
patlak burst, flat (tire)
pazar Sunday, market
peçete table napkin
pek very, much
pekala, peki, pekiyi
   very well, OK, very
   good, all right
pek çok very much

pencere window
penisilin penicillin
piyano piano
plaj beach
poliklinik
   clinic, clinic for out-
   patients
polis police
pompa pump
porsiyon portion
posta mail, postal service
postacı mailman
posta pulu postage stamp
posta memuru
   post office clerk
posta kutusu mailbox
postahane post office
program program
pul stamp
puslu hazy, misty

radyo radio
raket racket
reçete prescription
renk color
renkli colored
resepsiyon reception
resepsiyoncu receptionist
resim picture, drawing
resim çizmek to draw, to
   sketch
restoran restaurant
röntgen filmi X ray
rüzgar wind, breeze
rüzgarlı windy
rüzgar esmek to blow
   (wind)

saat hour, time
saat kaç? what time is it?
saat kaçta? At what
   time? When?
sabah morning
sabahleyin in the
   morning
sağ right
sağa to the right
sağda on the right side
sağdan from the right
   side
saha court, field, ground
(tenis sahası tennis
   court
basketbol sahası
   basketball court)

saman nezlesi hay fever
sanat art, craft
sanatçı (sanatkar)
   artisan, craftsman, artist
sanat müziği Turkish
   classical music
sanmak to suppose, to
   think
sandalye chair
sapmak to deviate, to
   turn
sarma wound, wrapped
satıcı seller
satın almak to buy, to
   purchase
satış selling
saz Turkish lute
semaver samovar
sen you (singular)
sende on you
senden from you
senin your, yours
seninle with you
seramik ceramic
sergi exhibition, show
servis service
sevilmek to be loved,
   liked
sevmek to love, to like
seyehat journey, travel
seyehat çeki traveler's
   check
seyretmek to watch
sıcak hot
sıfır zero
sigorta insurance
sinema cinema, movies
sırt back
sis fog, mist
sisli foggy, misty
siyah black, dark colored
siz you (plural, polite)
sizce according to you
size to you
sizde at you
sizden from you
sizin your, yours
sizinle with you
sürücü driver
soğuk cold
sokak road, street
sol left
sola to the left side

solda on the left side
soldan from the left side
son end, last
sonunda finally, in the end
sonra later, afterwards
soyadı last name
soyunmak to undress (oneself)
soyunma odası changing room
söylemek to say, to speak
spor sport
stadyum stadium
su water
su kayağı waterskiing
sulu boya watercolor (paint)
sunmak to present, to offer
sunulmak to be performed, presented
süper superb, extra better
sürmek to drive (a car), to take (time)
susmak to be silent, to be quiet
susamak to be thirsty, to thirst
susuz waterless, thirsty, dry
şahsi personal, private
şans luck
şanslı olmak to be lucky
şarap wine
şarkı song
şehir city
şeker sugar
şey thing
bir şey değil you're welcome, don't mention it
şimdi now
şirket company
şiş spit, skewer
şişe bottle, flask
şişmek to swell, to inflate
şöyle like that
şu that
şunlar those
şura that place

şurada in that place
şöför driver
taahhütlü registered (letter, etc.)
tabak plate, dish
taksi taxi
tam complete, exact, entire, whole
tamam complete, okay, correct, very well
tamir etmek (or yapmak) to repair, to fix
tane a single individual item
taraf side
tarih history
tanışmak to get acquainted with
tanıştırmak to introduce to one another
tartmak to weigh
tatil holiday
tavsiye etmek to recommend
taze fresh, new
tehlike danger, risk
tek a single item
tekerlek wheel (tire)
telefon telephone
telefonlu with a telephone
telefon etmek to phone
telefon kulübesi telephone booth
televizyon television
telgraf telegraph
temiz clean, pure
tenis tennis
tenis topu tennis ball
teras terrace
tercih etmek to prefer
tereyağı butter
terminal terminal
tesbih worry beads
teslim etmek to deliver, to hand over
teşekkür thanks
teşekkür etmek to thank
top ball
trafik traffic
trafik hastahanesi traffic accident hospital

trafik polisi traffic policeman
tren train
turist tourist
turist rehberi tour guide
turizm tourism
tutmak to total up, to come to . . .
tuvalet toilet
tuz salt
tükenmek to be exhausted, to run out
tünaydın good evening
ucuz cheap
uçak airplane
uçuş flight, flying
ulak courier
özel ulak special courier
uluslararası international
usta master (of a trade or craft)
uyumak to sleep, to go to sleep
uzak far away
uzun long, tall
uzun araç (TIR-kamyonu) truck
ücret price
ülke country
üzerine on, upon, on the subject of
üzülmek to be sorry
üzüm grape

vapur steamer, passenger boat
var to exist, to have
varmak to arrive at, to reach
vazo vase
ve and, also, too
vermek to give, to deliver
veya or
vezne cashier's office
vites gears (automobile)
vites kutusu gearbox (automobile)
voleybol volleyball
yağ oil, fat, butter
yağmak to rain
yağlı oily, fatty, in oil
yağlıboya oil paint

VOCABULARY

yağmur (yağmurlu) rain (rainy)
yağmur yağmak to rain
yağ pompası oil pump
yakmak to burn, to scorch
yakın near, nearby
yaklaşık approximately, about
yalnız alone, only
yan side
yangın fire
yangın söndürücü fire extinguisher
yanlış error, mistake, wrong
yanlışlık error, mistake, blunder
yapmak to do, to make
yaprak leaf
yaralı wounded, hurt
yardım help
yardım etmek to help
yarım half
yarın tomorrow
yasak prohibited, forbidden
yaşamak to live, to reside

yaşantı manner of living, life
yatak bed
yataklı furnished with a bed
yavaş slow, gentle
yavaşça slowly, gently
yaya pedestrian, passerby
yayla high plateau
yaz summer
yazın in the summer
yazlık for summer use
yazmak to write
yedek parça spare part
yelken sailboat
yelkencilik sailing
yemek food, meal
yemek yemek to eat
yeni new
yer place
yerine in place of, instead of
yetki authority
yetkili qualified, authorized person
yıl year

yok not to exist, not to have
yoksa if not, otherwise, or else
yol road
yolculuk travel, journey
yorucu tiring
yöntem method, way
yörük Turcoman
yukarı up, above, upwards
yün wool, woollen
yün iplik wool, yarn
yürümek to walk
yürüme walking
yürüyerek on foot, by walking
yüzmek to swim
yüzme havuzu swimming pool
yüzme simidi rubber ring

zengin rich
zeytin olive
ziyaret visit
iş ziyareti business visit
zor difficult